DEUTERONOMIC HISTORY

INTERPRETING BIBLICAL TEXTS

INTERPRETING **ibt** BIBLICAL TEXTS

Deuteronomic History

Terence E. Fretheim

LLOYD R. BAILEY, SR.
and
VICTOR P. FURNISH, EDITORS

ABINGDON PRESS   NASHVILLE

DEUTERONOMIC HISTORY

Copyright © 1983 by Abingdon Press

This book is printed on recycled, acid-free paper.

Library of Congress Cataloging in Publication Data

FRETHEIM, TERENCE E.
      Deuteronomic history.
      (Interpreting Biblical texts)
      Bibliography: p.
      1. Bible, O.T. Former Prophets—Criticism, interpretation,
      etc. I. Bailey, Lloyd R. II. Furnish, Victor Paul. III. Title.
      IV. Series.
      BS1286.5.F73   1983   222   82-20593

ISBN 0-687-10497-1

Unless otherwise indicated, Scripture quotations are from the Revised Standard
Common Bible, copyrighted © 1973 by the Division of Christian Education,
National Council of Churches, and are used by permission.

Scripture quotations marked TEV are from the Bible in Today's English (Good
News for Modern Man). Copyright © American Bible Society, 1966, 1971, 1976,
and are used by permission.

Scripture quotations marked JB are from The Jerusalem Bible, copyright © 1966
by Darton, Longman & Todd, Ltd. and Doubleday & Company, Inc., and are
used by permission.

93 94 95 96 97 98 99 00 01 02 — 13 12 11 10 9 8 7 6 5

MANUFACTURED IN THE UNITED STATES OF AMERICA

INTERPRETING BIBLICAL TEXTS:
Editors' Foreword

The volumes in this series have been planned for those who are convinced that the Bible has meaning for our life today, and who wish to enhance their skills as interpreters of the biblical texts. Such interpreters must necessarily engage themselves in two closely related tasks: (1) determining as much as possible about the original meaning of the various biblical writings, and (2) determining in what respect these texts are still meaningful today. The objective of the present series is to keep both of these tasks carefully in view, and to provide assistance in relating the one to the other.

Because of this overall objective it would be wrong to regard the individual volumes in this series as commentaries, as homiletical expositions of selected texts, or as abstract discussions of "the hermeneutical problem." Rather, they have been written in order to identify and illustrate what is involved in relating the meaning of the biblical texts in their own times to their meaning in ours. Biblical commentaries and other technical reference works sometimes focus exclusively on the first paying little or no attention to the second. On the other hand, many attempts to expound the contemporary "relevance" of biblical themes or passages pay scant attention to the intentions of the texts themselves. And although one of the standard topics of "hermeneutics" is how a text's original meaning relates to its present meaning, such discussions often employ highly technical philosophical language and proceed with little reference to concrete examples. By way of contrast, the present volumes are written in language that will be understood by scholars, clergy and laypersons alike, and they deal with concrete texts, actual problems of interpretation, and practical procedures for moving from "then" to "now."

Each contributor to this series is committed to three basic tasks: (1) a description of the salient features of the particular type of biblical literature or section of the canon assigned to him; (2) the identification and explanation of the basic assumptions that guide his analysis and explication of those materials; and (3) the discussion of possible contemporary meanings of representative texts, in view of the specified assumptions with which the interpreter approaches them. Considerations that should be borne in mind by the interpreter in reflecting upon contemporary meanings of these texts are introduced by the sign ● and are accentuated with a different size of type.

The assumptions that are brought to biblical interpretation may vary from one author to the next, and will undoubtedly differ from those of many readers. Nonetheless, we believe that the present series, by illustrating how careful interpreters carry out their tasks, will encourage readers to be more reflective about the way they interpret the Bible.

Lloyd Bailey
Duke Divinity School

Victor Paul Furnish
Perkins School of Theology
Southern Methodist University

PREFACE

Given the current emphasis on story in theology and preaching, the deuteronomic history should prove to be a veritable gold mine of a resource. These texts are filled with stories that reflect the complexities and ambiguities of the life of the people of God. As such, God's people today should be able to find a "home" here, for life's issues have remained remarkably constant through the generations. Thus, a Word of God addressed then may become a Word addressed now.

Given the focus on story, as well as the continuing interest in revelation in history matters, it's surprising that there are not more texts from these books represented in the lectionaries (seven are presented here). This may well reflect a comparative neglect of certain dimensions of these texts by scholars over the years. It has only been recently that scholars have begun to delve into these texts with interest beyond the overarching historiographical and traditio-historical ones. The new literary criticism especially promises that new depths will be plumbed in years to come. It's to be hoped that those who construct lectionaries will be paying close attention to such developments.

I wish to express my appreciation to my colleagues at Luther Northwestern Seminary for their helpful discussions, and to Editor Lloyd Bailey for his encouragement and insight. Finally, I wish to thank Aid Association for Lutherans for their financial assistance along the way.

CONTENTS

INTRODUCTION

Faith, Criticism, and "Application"

For the last two centuries, and more, the Bible has been the subject of a revolution. The essence of the upheaval has had to do with the effects of the claim that the biblical writings are *historical* materials. That is to say, they can be fully understood only in the light of the historical periods in which they were produced. Hence the shorthand phrase: historical criticism. While this phrase traditionally has been used to encompass literary-critical matters as well, it is now more common to distinguish sharply between literary and historical criticism as two separate, but complementary, approaches to the text.

The fundamental purpose of historical and literary criticism is to let the text speak for itself, by providing as many angles of vision on it as possible. The concern of the method is to preserve the integrity of the text. Finally, however, it will assist us more in determining what the text does *not* say than what it does say.

A few negative reactions to a historical-critical approach have been occasioned by the way in which some interpreters have defined and/or used the method. But, contrary to the opinion of critics, the use of historical-critical tools is not bound to an "objectivistic" approach, or to the view that history is a closed continuum in which there is no room for divine activity. Such tools may also be used hand in hand with a concern to clarify the theological dimension which all biblical materials contain.

Personal presuppositions, beliefs, and perspectives are really much more pervasive in biblical study than most of us realize. Believers often differ radically in their understanding of certain texts, and the reason is most often due to the "baggage" we bring with us to the study of the text. Our value system, sacramental theology, philosophy of history, socioeconomic background, religious upbringing, literary theories, and a host of other matters will powerfully affect our biblical interpretation. While we do have some powers to realize this fact and to guard against it, we will always be influenced by our traditions, our experiences, and, perhaps above all, by what is really absorbing us at the moment.

It is well to be reminded that modern literary or historical approaches to a text also do not provide a "neutral" place to stand in the process of interpretation. All approaches and all questions are contemporary approaches and questions; they are informed by presuppositions of one kind or another that affect exegetical results. Consequently, the "original meaning" of the text or the "intention" of the author are no longer discoverable in anything approaching a pure form. We do need to be concerned about determining, as far as possible, how a text may have functioned in its ancient setting(s), i.e., about the issues or questions of the community to which the text was responding (cf. pp. 44ff.). Yet, we must recognize that the "meaning" which we will perceive will be determined not simply by what we find out about the situation of the text's origin, but also by the conglomerate of meanings and effects that the text has had over the years, all of which affect us when we talk about "meaning."

Yet, this is not an occasion for despair or for a frantic search for objectivity. The *positive* role of past biblical interpretation and contemporary experience should be recognized. Even more, given the fact that the original writers were not neutral and "objective," the more detached we seek to be when we read the text, the less likely we will be to hear it in the way that they intended. Or, to put that point positively, the more committed we are to the faith claims of the text, the more in tune we are apt to be to its full meaning. Such a predisposition enables us to come to terms with more than externals; it enables a greater participation in the fullness of the reality that the text describes. If we take the biblical God seriously and the experience of the people of God as our own, we do not remain a spectator or an investigator who keeps the text at arm's length. To study the text with explicit theological, or philosophical, commitments will often make for significant exegetical insight.

But does this approach not open the door to subjectivity with respect to the results of exegesis, so that "anything goes"? Given the inevitable role of subjectivity, are there not objective controls available so that the text is not overpowered by, or confused with, our pre-understanding? Careful attention to the following matters will indeed enable a greater subjective/ objective balance to emerge.

1. Be attentive to the canons of accountability which have been developed in each of the biblical disciplines, particularly in historical criticism. Such canons provide checks upon our work. These canons are public, and generally agreed upon in such areas as text criticism, form criticism, etc. To use them is to recognize the important role of community in assessing interpretations. Not as commonly known, perhaps, are those canons that have been developed for theological work, namely, questions of intelligibility and coherence, questions of appropriateness in relation to the text and its traditions, and questions of adequacy relative to common human experience, and to the issues being addressed.

2. Learn to know and acknowledge what our most basic predispositions and perspectives are. And, then, read widely among the works of those who come from different backgrounds and traditions. This, too, provides for bringing the wisdom of the larger community (within and without the community of faith) to bear upon our interpretive work. This will help prevent the perpetuation of a closed understanding of the Bible, and

challenge us to revise, broaden, and deepen our presently held ideas about the text.

One basic result of this process is that the text, the interpreter, and the latter's situation vis-à-vis the people of God will illumine one another. A dialogue will emerge wherein the text, tradition, criticism, and contemporary experience are constantly intersecting, and out of that mix important insights into the meaning of the text can commonly emerge.

Thus, there is a sense in which the word "application" is one of the demons at work in our interpretation of texts. It suggests that the first task is historical, descriptive, objective; then, with that material in hand, we move to an application of the text to a contemporary situation. However, given the intersections noted above, this two-step approach to the text belies what actually happens in the course of interpretation. But, what if we began biblical study with the assumption that we are not to be concerned with "application" at all? This approach is worth exploring. Rather than seeking to apply the text, or seeking to *make* it relevant to today, you assume that it *is* relevant and that the task is to enable that relevance to be seen, or, in other language, to facilitate the urgency of the text as it intersects with individual lives and situations.

Some texts are more immediate with respect to meaning than are others, and this depends upon a variety of factors, including who the readers/hearers are, and what their experiences in and out of the community of faith have been. Take Psalm 23 as one example. If you are ministering to a lifelong Christian whose spouse has just died, there will be an immediacy with respect to meaning because of its intersection with a certain life experience. It may even be that an attempt at commentary will obscure or limit that meaning. Perhaps the best you can do is restate the psalm in different words, yet chances are you will not be saying anything new, but only reinforcing or reminding the bereaved of what is already known. Thus, you are not applying the text to a life situation at all. The text itself applies; the intersection with life experience gives it an immediacy that makes unnecessary any two-step approach.

Other texts, e.g., Joshua 6, will not be as immediate to hearers, largely because it lacks intersection with their life experience. There will, in fact, be a wide range of immediacy as you move across biblical texts, but the basic task of the interpreter remains the same throughout: to work with a text in such a fashion that it comes to have a greater immediacy to the hearer. The fundamental task is to talk about the text in language that constantly intersects with the hearer's experience, and thus the meaning of the text will be "there" for them, apart from any specific "application."

Moreover, the hearer's perception of what has happened will be quite different from the normal application method. This is so because the hearer is left, not with *your* interpretation of the text in some secondary or applied fashion and somehow abstracted from the text, but with the *text itself* whose meaning has become immediate to their own life experience. Thus, the text is not an object, something that is tinkered with and talked about as something "back then" which is now being applied, but rather it is direct address. The goal, of course, is to enable people to hear the text and not merely a sermon on the text, so that they will say, finally, that the text rather than the sermon spoke to them.

As far as study of the text is concerned, then, the basic relationship to it should be in terms of a conversation, an asking and a listening that is open to the faith claims of the text, and with contemporary experience in view, and this, not as some capstone after your more objective analysis of the text, but at every stage of your study.

The Deuteronomic History

The deuteronomic (or deuteronomistic) history is a shorthand designation of fairly recent vintage for the books of Joshua, Judges, Samuel, and Kings, with Deuteronomy often recognized as the introduction to them. It has been common to refer to these books as "The Former Prophets" because of the important role the prophetic word plays in the narrative. Perhaps most commonly, however, the general label of "Historical Books" has been given to them, because of their obvious concern to relate the history of Israel from the entrance into the land to the time of the Babylonian exile. A few observations regarding composition, authorship, date, structure, and general character are important for the subsequent discussion.

Composition, authorship, and date. Traditionally, the individual books of the corpus have been treated in isolation from one another, with single, unknown authors reporting on recent events. Over the last two hundred years, however, two major theories regarding the composition of these books has emerged in biblical scholarship.

First, there has been the attempt to tie them closely to the Pentateuch, and thus to see Genesis through Kings as one comprehensive history. That is, it has been thought that the major sources of the Pentateuch (JEDP) originally continued through these materials. This was thought to be particularly clear in the case of Joshua, where the fulfillment of the promises to the Patriarchs regarding the land is reported. (Hence all six were designated as the Hexateuch.) Yet, this hypothesis has not maintained wide acceptance, largely because no consensus has emerged regarding the scope of the individual sources, and because insufficient account was given thereby for the pervasiveness of the deuteronomic style and outlook in these books. It is this latter observation which has led to a second proposal, to which most scholars today subscribe in one form or another.

Taking their cue from the prominent deuteronomic imprint on these books, scholars have come to see Joshua–Kings as an independent historical work, with Deuteronomy as an introduction. (This reduces the Pentateuch to a Tetrateuch, Genesis–Numbers.) This perspective not only helps explain the literary and theological connections to Deuteronomy, but also the virtual absence of deuteronomic material in Genesis–Numbers, as well as the double introduction to the book of Deuteronomy (1:1–4:43; 4:44ff.). In the classic formulation by Martin Noth in 1943, it was thought that this work was put together by an author living in the exilic period (587–539 B.C.) who gathered together a variety of oral and written traditions and wove them into a comprehensive whole.

While this hypothesis has gained wide acceptance in its general form, certain problems have occasioned refinements in its formulation. Foremost among these difficulties is the change in approach which may be observed at the end of 2 Kings: there is an absence of the typical theological reflection upon important events, in this case, upon the destruction of Jerusalem. Thus, a hypothesis has emerged which speaks of two stages of editing (a "dual redaction") of the historical work: a major one by an apologist for the reform of Josiah (around 620 B.C.) and a minor one during the exile which stresses the just judgment of God and brings the work up to date (the last verses report an event of 561 B.C.).

We cannot be certain whether the editors were country preachers (Levites), a prophetic school, or leaders standing within the Jerusalemite tradition but influenced by northern materials. (The last seems most likely.) Whether the final redactor lived in Palestine or Babylon is uncertain.

It is important to note that, even if the dual redaction hypothesis proves to be the most convincing, it is necessary to understand how the *entire* history may have functioned in the exilic context. That will be our concern in this volume. Because it is the exilic redactor through whose hands the material was finally passed, we have to reckon with how the material would have functioned in that situation. While the exilic redactor may have added to an earlier work, that is not the only editing technique that was available for use. He/they may also have omitted or rearranged traditions to reflect the concerns of that era. Finally, however, we can never be certain that the present selection and arrangement of materials is anything other than a single exilic one, though certain materials within the collection may be discerned by their content as preexilic in origin.

It is clear that the redactor(s) of this work did not create a history of Israel out of whole cloth. They inherited a variety of types of literature from the past, and such materials make up the bulk of the history. Some of these sources are explicitly referred

to in the narrative (cf. Josh 10:13; 1 Kgs 11:41; 2 Kgs 16:19).
Some materials appear to be self-contained and isolatable from
their context, and hence may well have come to the redactor's
hand in a form much like we now have them (e.g., the ark
narrative in 1 Samuel 4–6; the tribal allotment list in Joshua
13–21; cf. pp. 122-48).

There was considerable diversity in perspective in these
inherited traditions, which the editors chose to retain, and they
worked them over in different ways. That is why certain periods
were virtually ignored (e.g., the reign of Omri), while others
were described at length (e.g., those of Elijah and Elisha).
Certain materials were edited in recognizable regularity (e.g.,
the reigns of the kings), while others were given little editorial
attention (e.g., 1 Samuel 13–31). This may suggest that a variety
of editors (a school) were at work on the material, having a
common perspective overall, but working with different editorial
principles. In this light, it is my view that the dual redaction
hypothesis is too simple, as if there were two theoretically
discoverable dates on which the editions of the total history were
published. It seems to me more likely, especially in view of this
diversity, that there was a school at work on these traditions over
a number of generations, perhaps from the time of King
Hezekiah (715-687 B.C.) onward. Thus, the concerns of a number
of eras are reflected in the completed work, and yet the final
stamp is decisively exilic. (The latter is the only redactional stage
of which we can be absolutely certain.)

Basic Concerns. The purpose of this work is basically hortatory
(exhortation), and in that sense it is continuous with the book of
Deuteronomy, which is often described as "preached law."

While key themes recur throughout, giving a certain overall
perspective to the work, cautions are in order. An attempt to
isolate one major theme would certainly force the work into a
mold for which it was not designed. With its hortatory agenda, a
variety of issues and themes is expressed, no doubt correspond-
ing in significant ways to the complexities of the community for
which it was intended. Moreover, the variety of the inherited
traditions will inevitably make for no little thematic diversity.

These various themes ought not be viewed as in competition with one another, but as complementary. At the same time, taken as a group, they will give a certain theological direction to the work as a whole.

Some sorting out of key thematic elements might be helpful. It is striking to note the utterly pessimistic outlook that M. Noth (1943) perceived in the work. For him, the corpus was designed only to show that God's actions leading to the destruction of Israel and Judah were justified. Thus, the past was used only in order to explain the present, and no hope was articulated for the future. Such a bleak picture is seldom maintained today, although the dark elements in the narrative cannot be dismissed.

A more balanced picture emerged with the work of Gerhard von Rad (1953, 1962). He understood the materials not fundamentally to be a history of Israel, but to be an account of the word of God as it functioned within the ongoing life of Israel. Thus, "Yahweh's word is active in the history of Judah, creating that history, and that in a double capacity: (1) as law, judging and destroying; (2) as gospel, i.e., in the David prophecy, which was constantly being fulfilled—saving and forgiving" (1953, p. 89). The former is largely the word of God, which derived from Moses and the prophets; their warnings were clear and unmistakable, and because they were ignored this led to the death of both the southern and the northern kingdoms. But, interwoven with this word of judgment is the promise to David (articulated esp. in 2 Samuel 7) which provided hope, indeed a "messianic hope," for the people in all times of difficulty, even in the death of exile. Thus, there is a fusion of the Mosaic and Davidic traditions, and the result is a relatively simple message for the people of God: Repent, and trust God's promise, which will not fail. The instructional and hortatory language make sense only if there is hope for the future. In terms of an overarching perspective, von Rad's remains the most satisfactory today.

H. W. Wolff (1961) emphasized the repentance theme, and demonstrated the important role it played in key passages (e.g., 1 Kgs 8:46-53). He would disagree with von Rad, however, regarding the specific character of the hope. Wolff would stress that certain passages (e.g., 1 Kgs 2:3-4; 9:5-7) make the Davidic covenant conditional upon obedience, and because of the kings' disobedience, this covenant was no longer in force. Hence, uncertainties reign at the end of 2 Kings (25:27-30), which contains no allusion to any Davidic covenant. In the absence of any specific hope, Israel could only trust that, given God's response to repentant people in the past, there would be a comparable response in the future; God would hear and forgive (1 Kgs 8:34ff.). At the same time, the repentance of the people would not be accomplished in some "bootstrap" fashion, as if they have the wherewithall within themselves to return to God. God is so much at work in them that repentance is finally as much a divine act as a human one; in fact, because of God's involvement, such repentance, itself, constitutes a gift of God (Deut 4:29-31; 30:1-10; 1 Kgs 8:58).

This perspective is basically the same as that of von Rad, though with a stronger emphasis upon repentance, and a diminishing of the promise, particularly in its messianic shape. While one might agree in large part with this refinement, Wolff does not give sufficient emphasis to the promise, since repentance is possible only if the promise is in view. Repentance is not presented in the text as a naked demand, which Israel is somehow expected to obey on her own with no consciousness of God's work in her life (see 1 Kgs 8:56-57). Rather, encouragement to repent is set against the background of God's commitment to Israel and the terrible speed of mercy, heretofore. The conditioning of the Davidic covenant to which Wolff points has now been demonstrated to be limited in scope (see Nelson, 1981), and the ending of Kings represents uncertainty only with respect to the shape which fulfillment might take. (See our study of 2 Samuel 7 below.) God's promise is not conditional, either to David or to people. The narrative is too punctuated with statements to the contrary. For example:

For the Lord your God is a merciful God; he will not fail you or destroy you or forget the covenant with your fathers which he swore to them (Deut 4:31).

> I will never break my covenant with you (Judg 2:1).
>
> For the Lord will not cast away his people (1 Sam 12:22).
>
> Your throne shall be established forever (2 Sam 7:16).

God's promises will not fail; they will never be made null and void, as far as God is concerned. Though a rebellious generation might not live to see the fulfillment of the promise, because they have rejected God, the promise can be relied on. Thus, the promise is an everlasting one, though participation in its fulfillment is not *guaranteed* to every person or generation. The promise is always there for the believing to cling to, and they know that God will ever be at work to fulfill it.

Within this framework, it is my thesis that the first (and second, in the reformed numbering) commandment (i.e., Deut 5:7-10), together with a certain understanding of God, constitutes the heart of the concern of the deuteronomic historian.

A key question raised by the exiles is stated in 1 Kgs 9:8, and Deut 29:24 ff.: "Why has the Lord done thus to this land and to this house?"

The question is answered: "Because they forsook the Lord their God who brought their fathers out of the land of Egypt, and laid hold on other gods, and worshiped them and served them; therefore the Lord has brought all this evil upon them." The focus of the response is on unfaithfulness to God, manifested fundamentally in the worship of other gods. The present situation in exile is thus due, not to a God whose promises have proved to be unreliable, but to Israel's failure to be faithful to the God who has made the promise.

The problem is, thus, fundamentally a matter of faith and unfaith, and not of obedience and disobedience vis-à-vis an external code. Sometimes, scholars speak of the apostasy of Israel in legalistic terms, as if it were finally a problem of not measuring up to an external code of conduct. Failure to keep the commandments, however, is seen by the deuteronomic historian to be symptomatic of a more pervasive problem, namely, disloyalty to God. This can be illustrated from many texts, but perhaps 2 Kgs 17:7-18 is most striking: all the specific sins cited have to do with the service of other gods. The heart of the matter is that they "did not believe in the Lord their God" (v 14). To "forsake *all* the commandments of the Lord their God" (v 16) finds its definition in terms of idolatry. The reform of Josiah is also illustrative of this point (2 Kgs 23:4-25): every one of the covenant reforms instituted by this faithful king had to do with the service of other gods. The concern for the centralization of worship in Jerusalem, and the repeated assertion that "the sin of Jeroboam" was an important criterion of judgment, was not because of some bureaucratic legalism perpetrated by Jerusalem officialdom, but because of the temptation to idolatry. Thus, centralization was a means to another end, a way of safeguarding the essential concerns of the first commandment (cf. the discussion of Joshua 24).

A focus on the first commandment is also evident in the use of covenant language. It is often suggested that Israel's understanding of the Sinai covenant was based upon analogy with international political treaties of the suzerainty type. However, such dependence, in the case of the deuteronomic historian, is much less than is commonly claimed, particularly in drawing out theological implications of the covenant. As we shall see, the historian makes it abundantly clear that God is not bound to react to the people in some schematic or univocal fashion. The relationship between God and people is much too personally oriented, has too much flexibility in it, for contractual language to do it justice. God's mercy and compassion go beyond simple justice, again and again. God is not bound by form in responding; his actions are not legalistically defined or determined in advance.

The language of "forsaking" the covenant is oriented, almost exclusively, in terms of the first commandment. "It is because they forsook the covenant of the Lord . . . and went and served other gods and worshiped them" (Deut 29:25-26); "If you transgress the covenant of the Lord your God . . . and go and serve other gods" (Josh 23:16; cf. Deut 17:2-3; 31:16, 20; Judg 2:20; 1 Kgs 11:9-11; 2 Kgs 17:15). As we will see in our discussion of Joshua 24, the making of the covenant in v 25 has solely to do with a first commandment orientation (cf. 2 Kgs 17:35-38), as does the essential meaning of the covenant in 2 Kings 23 (cf. above).

If the Sinai (Mosaic) covenant is so understood, then the relationship between it and the covenant which God establishes with David (and with the people) loses much (but not all) of its tension. The former, which the people transgress, is most commonly referred to as "my covenant," i.e., God's covenant, as is the latter (Judg 2:1). If "both" covenants were initiated and established by God, it could then appear to the historian that there is finally only one covenant, viewed from different angles. From the divine side, the focus is on promise; from the human side the focus is on the first commandment, or, in other language, on faith and trust in God alone. Thus, the only "condition" of the latter is finally faith and trust. At times, the stress is placed on the divine promise to the patriarchs (e.g., Deut 4:31; 29:12-13; 2 Kgs 13:23) and David (2 Sam 7; 23:5), while at other times it is on the importance of the human response of faith and trust (cf. passages noted above). Thus, it would appear that the historian, in weaving together the Abrahamic-Davidic/Sinaitic-Shechemite traditions about covenant, takes a step beyond the original Deuteronomy (chaps. 5–28). He views these covenants as two sides of the same coin; he keeps the promise and repentance/faith inextricably intertwined.

At the same time, it is possible that Deuteronomy makes a comparable distinction between "command" (singular) and "statutes and ordinances" (cf. 5:31; 6:1; 17:20; 30:11). The command is the first commandment (5:7-10), defined in other terms in 6:5: "You shall love the Lord your God with all your heart, and with all your soul, and with all your might" (cf. 5:10, "who love me"). This is a call to be faithful to God, to have no other gods. The opposite of this is, thus, not disobedience of some external code, but a faithless rejection of God as Lord.

What, then, of the relationship between command and commandments? The latter are secondary, answering the question: How should one's faithfulness to God be expressed in the "ins and outs" of daily life at this particular time and place?

While the command remains constant, permanent, unchanging, the way in which the command expresses itself in daily life may vary according to the life situation (and hence the adaptation of the commandments through the years).

In this connection, it should be noted that it is not disobedience of individual commandments that constitutes the threat to life for Israel; it is unfaithfulness to God, the serving of other gods (manifested in life in a pervasive lack of concern for the various commandments). Hence, the fundamental call to the people, when the latter has occurred, is not that they should obey individual commandments, but to put away other gods and return to the Lord.

This fundamental concern of the deuteronomic history is expressed in a variety of language. The language of "serving" and "fearing" indicates the centrality of the personal loyalty issue (see Josh 24:14ff.; 1 Sam 7:3, 12:20, 24). Also common are "walking before the Lord" or "following him" (cf. 1 Kgs 2:4; 3:6; 8:23-25; 1 Kgs 11:4-5).

Passages such as Joshua 1 (see our chapter below) show that notions of gift and promise provide the context for any talk about commandments. It is, first of all, God's electing and saving action which constitutes relationship. Obedience to commandments is a concern that derives from an already established relationship, rather than the basis for establishing that relationship. Hence, a call to obedience invites the people to a life which will be true to that relationship. Moreover, obedience cannot maintain or preserve (or reestablish) the relationship, since it was not constitutive of the relationship in the first place. Moreover, while one can more fully realize the existing relationship through obedience, because of sin one cannot finally preserve it. Disobedience, on the other hand, is a sign that there is something wrong with the relationship with God. Because of Israel's lack of faith and trust in God alone (which would issue in disobedient actions of various sorts), the covenant relationship is endangered and, finally, capable of fracture. But, such a result is not inevitable, since God in mercy and patience could preserve the relationship in spite of such disloyalty (and did, in fact, again and again). As 1 Kings 8 makes clear, on the basis of what God has done and promised (vv 15-26), forgiveness is available to the sinful community when it repents (vv 27-53). Nowhere is obedience of commandments recognized as a basis upon which forgiveness and restoration of relationship is granted.

Finally, it might be noted that the commandments, themselves, are perceived to be a gracious gift of God. They are given "that it may go well with you, and with your children after you, and that you may prolong your days in the land which the Lord your God gives you forever" (Deut 4:40; cf. Josh 1:8-9; 1 Kgs 2:3). The commandments were given for life, with the best interests of God's people in mind. The motive clause language, "obey . . . that it might go well with you," is often misunderstood in terms of rewards. Rather, an *intrinsic* relationship is perceived between obedience to the commandments and life. That is to say, obedience to the commandments, just by virtue of their being obeyed, will make for a better life. This is not understood in some mechanical or automatic way, as if such results were inevitable. But, this will be the normal outcome of obedience. Thus, promises of life, and success, and prosperity are not seen as rewards, but as the normal results of obedience, given the moral order which God has established and perpetuates (see Deut 30:8-10).

Alongside the response of unbelief on the part of the people is a striking picture of God (cf. the discussion in the chapter on Judges 2). God is revealed as anything but one who is impatient, or capricious, or who is adhering to some retributionary scheme. Rather, God is one who has proven faithful to promises given to the fathers and is a source of blessings without end, though the people have often proved faithless (cf. Deut 9:4-5). God is revealed as one who has been willing to make adjustments in ways of working with people, always taking new initiatives in dealing with negative situations (e.g., the monarchy). There have been warnings of the consequences of unbelief again and again, particularly through the prophets who, out of sheer mercy, have been raised up to speak to the people. God is one who has been "moved to pity" time and again, giving Israel another chance to turn away from their disloyalties to their creator and redeemer. He will respond to his people's cries for help, or act mercifully entirely on his own initiative (1 Samuel 24; Judges 2; 2 Kgs 13:23). And even, finally, when it is seen that disaster must fall, this is cast in terms of death, but not eternal death or annihilation, for judgment is perceived throughout the history as a refining fire, as a means by which life might finally come again (cf. Deut 4:26-31). No word of final rejection is pronounced. The persistent pattern of promise and fulfillment throughout the narrative should make it clear to the exiles that this kind of God is the only basis for hope. All of God's actions are directed to one goal: "That you might know that the Lord is God; there is no other besides him" (Deut 4:35, 39; 30:6). It is finally this picture of God that is the interpretive key to the whole history of Israel.

One of the reasons why some scholars have advocated a two-stage editorial development for the deuteronomic history (e.g., Cross, 1973, Nelson) is that they detect theological tensions within the work. For example, they consider the reiteration of the unconditional promise to David to stand in too jarring a tension with strong notes of curse, particularly the inevitable punishment announced for Manasseh's sins (2 Kgs 23:26-27). There may well be conflicting theological perspectives within the history as a whole, but this ought not be considered one of them. As is noted below in the study of 2 Samuel 7, there is no theological contradiction between the theme of death-dealing judgment, and that of promise, and the presence of the latter theme does not necessarily mean optimism in the midst of judgment (witness Lamentations, or Psalm 89). As will be noted in the study on Judges 2–3, it is in fact one of God's ways with the people that they must pass through death in order to receive life. At the end of 2 Kings death has been experienced, and nearly overwhelms the narrative. Nevertheless, no final rejection is stated; the promise continues to be articulated. Even a return from exile is hardly contemplated, so uncertain is the shape of the future. Thus, whatever conclusion one might have regarding the redactional history of these books, it is clear that a strong note of judgment and a continued affirmation of promise live together in exile, in the minds of those "who wait for him . . . wait quietly for the salvation of the Lord . . . for the Lord will not cast off forever" (Lam 3:25-31; cf. pp. 119-20).

Finally, it might be noted that scholars have stressed a number of other themes, largely within the framework noted above. Two might be noted. Brueggemann (1968) sees a recurring concern for "the good," primarily in terms of that faithfulness and graciousness of God which serve to draw the people to repentance. D. McCarthy (1965, 1974) perceives a recurrent theme of wrath, as well as an ongoing concern about proper leadership, since it so affects the relationship between God and people. Because the problems of political and religious continuity were so considerable during the Exile, one can see how this concern was retained or lifted up for attention. It will emerge throughout the studies that follow.

Historiography: Did It Happen?

The books of the deuteronomic history are commonly referred to as the historical books. This traditional designation arose because the narratives give the appearance of being a straightforward account of the history of Israel from the conquest of the land to the fall of Jerusalem some 700 years later. Upon closer inspection, however, one recognizes that the designation "historical narrative" is not accurate for all of these materials. For example, Judg 9:7-15 constitutes a fable, and 2 Sam 12:1-6 contains a parable. No blanket designation can be made regarding these books as a whole. Every text needs to be examined in, and of, itself in order to determine its relationship to what actually happened. Sometimes the answer is easy, as with the examples just noted; at other times the response is much more difficult. For example, to what degree does Joshua 6 portray an actual destruction of the city of Jericho? Or, did Samson really kill an army singlehandedly?

It is important that we discuss this matter in detail, not least because many individuals may get uneasy over what appears to be a hasty, or even cavalier, treatment of the problem. How do scholars go about determining the extent to which a narrative reflects something that actually happened? How important for faith is the "happenedness" of the events reported in the Bible? We shall take these questions in turn.

The historian who seeks to reconstruct the history of Israel from biblical texts is confronted with four interrelated problems:

1. The problem of the *selection of the material,* and the principles which have governed such selection. Every last detail of the known history of any period will not have been recorded. A selection will have been made. Some principles, examined or unexamined, will have determined what was thought important enough to pass on, and what could be omitted. For example, we know from extra-biblical sources that a very important battle took place at Qarqar in 853 B.C. between Israel under Ahab, and Assyria, but no reference is made to it in the Bible.

2. The problem of *meaning.* One's understanding of history is not exhausted by a statement that something has occurred; in fact, one has not really said very much about an event by merely saying that it happened. It is only when one introduces the question of the meaning of an event that one introduces the possibility of relationship among events; otherwise, they will remain a series of unconnected occurrences. In fact, meaning is implied immediately when one speaks of such relationships. The historian seeks to discover and interpret meaning, and because the meaning of an event has to do with its relationship not only with events that are proximate but also with all subsequent events that follow in some way from it, the full meaning of an event is never finally available. The meaning of any event is always living, always being expanded upon, as one discovers new ways in which the event has had an impact upon subsequent history. Thus, for example, what is the meaning of the conquest of Canaan by the Israelites? The meaning of the event for the participants is one thing; the meaning of the event for subsequent interpreters (e.g., the deuteronomic historian) may be another; the meaning for us may be still another. But, in all cases, there should be basic continuities in meaning.

3. The problem of *point of view*. The texts and material artifacts which are available for the reconstruction of Israel's history have to be interpreted; their meaning is not immediately apparent. All who seek to interpret them will do so from their own particular perspective. The result is that there is no such thing as uninterpreted history. A member of the people of God (whether in ancient Israel or today) will interpret Israel's history differently from one who is not a member. One's own situation in history (e.g., theological perspectives, cultural traditions, etc.) will inevitably play a role in one's historical assessments. Thus, there will inevitably be a diversity of opinion regarding such matters, and no historian's perspective can ever stand without need of correction. Thus, historians should be as explicit as they possibly can with regard to the perspectives which have governed their interpretation, and be open to the possibility that their understanding might be enhanced, or corrected, by someone who approaches the texts from another perspective.

4. The problem of *fact*. Did the events of which the text speaks really happen as stated, or are they only said to have happened? How is "fact" to be related to the interpretation of an event? While, as we have indicated, history is never facts alone, but facts plus supplied meaning plus the person involved in interpretation, it is important for historians to sort through these components in such a way as to suggest, as best they can, what actually occurred in the course of Israel's history.

Given these problems, what particular issues should the historian address? Nine items may be mentioned.

1. The purpose of the biblical narratives. Were they, e.g., written to reconstruct the history of Israel in a fashion similar to a modern historian writing a history, of, say, the Civil War? It is clear that the biblical narrator did not have modern historiographical methods with which to work (e.g., the concern for tracking down and sorting out apparent differences in accounts of the same event). Hence, one ought not fault them from that angle for failing to meet modern standards. Yet, it is clear that there was some concern for recovering Israel's past, and with some chronological coherence. This is evident from the fact that the

deuteronomic history is written in such a way that there is a movement from an earlier period to a later one, in addition to having chronological references (e.g., 1 Kgs 11:42; 2 Kgs 17:1).

However, it would appear that their fundamental purpose was not historiographical, i.e., writing history for the sake of writing history; rather, their concerns were religious. It might be said that the biblical narrators used the materials at their disposal for theological (or kerygmatic-didactic) purposes. Their goal is to tell the story of the interaction between God and Israel in order to elicit a response from their audience. (See below for further comments on this matter.) This purpose is perhaps best seen in 2 Kgs 17:8ff., "And this was so, because . . ." The theological perspectives of the narrator are here acknowledged and seen to be the angle of vision from which the story has been told.

One result of this particular approach is that an event of considerable significance for a historiographer may be passed over with little or no notice (e.g., the battle of Qarqar). On the other hand, that which is important for theological reasons may be lifted up for special attention (e.g., the relationship between Elijah and Jezebel). Thus, if the purpose of a biblical writer was not historiographical, we ought not interpret the resultant narrative as if it were. If the authors were not interested in historical questions per se, then we, with our (legitimate) interest in historiographical matters, should recognize that as historians we are using these materials in a way in which they were not intended to be used. It should also be clear that we have no business introducing the category of "error" or "inaccuracy" in our assessment of the biblical narratives. That would be like accusing authors of Bible story books of "error" because they had used some imagination in the retelling of the biblical story for children. On the contrary, we should realize that their purposes were not historiographical from the start. It may be that the biblical narrators have, indeed, transmitted matters that do not correspond to the facts of a situation, but this ought to be evaluated in terms of the purpose of the narrator.

2. Contemporaneity of the records, i.e., the closeness of the

writing to the events about which it purports to speak. On the one hand, the closer the report is to the event, the more reliable it will be, generally speaking. On the other hand, closeness is not *necessarily* more trustworthy, since a true perspective on an event may not be available until some time has passed. But, the generally acknowledged fact that no portion of the records that speak of the pre-Davidic period can be shown to be older than David in their present form, indicates something of the care with which one must approach these materials for historiographical usage. Much of it has been filtered through the minds of individuals who were not directly involved in the events. Moreover, there is the general problem of what happens to traditions when they are passed down by word of mouth for generations, as was certainly the case with a significant portion of this material. While there is ample witness to the tenacity of the shapes taken by "oral literature," continued use and interpretation inevitably leads to expansion and contraction of the material. This makes access to the original time and place of reported events more difficult than is commonly imagined.

3. The criterion of dissimilarity, i.e., the degree to which a narrative speaks of matters that differ from those of any subsequent period. Thus the fact that the office of judge is unlike anything we know from later Israelite history, indicates that it was probably not read back into the narrative from the experience of a later period, and can be relied upon in a general way.

4. Intrinsic probability. This is tied to the question of the congruence of what is reported with what we know about the specific or general course of history from other sources. Does a report sound reasonable or not, recognizing that our understanding of "reasonableness" is determined largely by our own historical experience? Was Naaman cured of his leprosy (2 Kings 5)? Did the axe float on the water (2 Kgs 6:1-7)? The goal here is not to be too gullible or too skeptical, to allow for the unique and the miraculous, while being wary of a predisposition to resort too quickly to such categories.

5. The implications of the type of literature in which the

narrative is cast. While the fable of Judges 9, and the parable of
2 Samuel 12 are readily identifiable, a problem arises when
literary form is not so easily recognized, or the canons for
identification and interpretation are not commonly agreed upon.
Thus, e.g., the stories of Samson (Judges 13–16) are notoriously
difficult for the historian to assess, even though the category of
"legend" is commonly given to them. Even more complex is the
so-called Succession Narrative (2 Samuel 9–1 Kings 2), for years
recognized as the most "historical" of the narratives in the
deuteronomic history; recent studies have suggested that
scholars may have been more sanguine with regard to its
historicity than they ought to have been.

6. The etiological factor (concern for the origins of some
name, practice, or institution). For example, to what degree was
the story of the crossing of the Jordan in Joshua 3–4 shaped by (or
even composed to explain the origins of) the later use of twelve
stones in a liturgical celebration of that event (4:21-24)? Or, did
the story of Achan originate out of a concern to explain the
origins of "the great heap of stones" in the Valley of "Achor"
(Josh 7:26)? The degree to which such etiologies were a creative
factor in the formation of traditions is much discussed among
scholars. But, most would now say that the etiological factor was
not a controlling element in most of these narratives, but was
secondarily attached to already existent traditions (e.g., the last
sentence of Josh 7:26 was added to the story at a late date).
Hence, the presence of etiological material is not commonly a
reason for making a negative judgment regarding the historicity
of the entire story to which it is attached.

7. Multiple attestation, i.e., the existence of more than one
version of a story (doublets). Whenever such occur, it is very
helpful to compare them with one another in order to try to get at
the most original form of the story. Thus, e.g., Judg 1:1–2:5
contains an account of the settlement of Canaan parallel to, but
briefer than, the one found in Joshua. The major difficulty is the
incompleteness of the results in the former account (see Judg
1:19, 21, 27-29) compared to the latter (see Josh 21:43). Most

scholars would contend that the Judges account is less idealized than the one in Joshua (cf. p. 52).

8. The point of view of the author, i.e., is there evidence of a bent or a bias which might affect the way in which the author tells the story of the past? In writing a history of the American Civil War, there may be a sympathy toward either northern or southern interests, which will affect historical judgments to some degree. The fact that there were many tensions between North and South in Israel (in fact, a civil war for many decades in the period 921-722 B.C.) suggests that we should be alert for such differences as may manifest themselves in the literature for this reason. Thus, when the Chronicler, after the Exile, retold the story of 2 Samuel and 1–2 Kings, he gave very little attention to the place of the North in the history of the period. One might also see such regional differences reflected in the story about the establishment of the kingship in 1 Samuel 8–12, where pro-monarchical (southern?), and anti-monarchical (northern?) traditions may be interwoven with one another.

9. Congruity with reliable external evidence, i.e., with materials in written or artifactual form. This is similar to the multiple attestation category, except that the evidence is external to the biblical material and is commonly in non-written form (which also needs to be interpreted!). Does the external evidence corroborate, or stand in tension, with what is set forth in the biblical materials? For example, a number of cities are mentioned in Joshua 1–12 as having been destroyed by the invading Israelites. Archaeological excavations have shown that they were indeed destroyed in the 13th century B.C., which is an acceptable date. However, no evidence has been unearthed to show that Israel, rather than, say, the Philistines perpetrated the destruction. On the other hand, biblical reports of the destruction of the cities of Jericho and Ai (Joshua 6–7), and other sites, do not correspond very well (in some cases, not at all) with the archaeological evidence. This indicates something of the complexity of the task faced by the historian. Keys to proceeding correctly are: (a) the balanced use of internal (i.e., literary) and external (i.e., archaeological) evidence, with one type not being

allowed to predominate; and (b) to determine where the balance of probability lies. All historical judgments are judgments of probability, and so it is a matter of weighing the evidence to determine what is more or less probable. Thus, in the conquest narratives, it is generally recognized as probable that the Israelites had something to do with the destruction levels in, at least, some of the cities of Palestine, but no *details* in the biblical accounts have been corroborated, and many difficulties remain (cf. below on Joshua 6). All in all, it is wise to remember that archaeology does not prove the *truth* of the Bible, for while certain correspondences may be found, with respect to factual data, there can be no external corroboration of the *meaning* of that data. For example, archaeological data might indicate that Israel destroyed a given city at a given time, but it could not demonstrate whether God willed the event.

Perhaps these factors are a sufficient indication of the complexity of the task of assessing the biblical traditions for reconstructing the history of Israel. With so many possibilities for interpretation, it is inevitable that there will be a diversity of opinion on a variety of subjects, just as there will be in writing the history of any people.

We need now to return to an earlier question: How important for faith is the "happenedness" of the various events reported in the Bible? There are a few interpreters who would make no distinctions among biblical events at this point: the historicity of the Exodus and axe-head stories, e.g., carrying equal weight for faith. Yet, such an approach stands in contradiction to the approach of the biblical writers themselves. Both Old Testament and New Testament writers give us warrant to make distinctions among events: they isolate certain key events as being constitutive of the community and hence important for faith, while other events are not given such significance. Such constitutive events (e.g., the Exodus) have been incorporated into confessional statements (e.g., Deut 26:5-9) and integrated again and again into the community's materials of faith (e.g., 1 Kgs 8:14ff.), while other events (e.g., 2 Kgs 6:1-7) are not given a central place. Hence, the pervasiveness of reference to an event, and the degree to which that event is believed to be constitutive of the community, serve to indicate whether its "happenedness" is important for faith.

The end result with respect to the deuteronomic history, without going into detail, is that it contains a very mixed set of materials from an historiographical point of view. It is clear that these materials are rooted decisively in the period from about 1200 to 561 B.C. At varying levels they reflect what happened to Israel, and in Israel, during this period. Moreover, they are reflective of what thoughtful Israelites considered the meaning(s) of those events to be at various times during this era. In such a reflective process, the authors and editors no doubt used their imagination freely (e.g., when they put forward the actual words of a private conversation).

As far as our use of these texts today is concerned, we are dealing with the story of a real people in particular times and places. The authors were not historiographers in any modern sense, however. They were fundamentally concerned about the religious meaning of events, and thus the material has value for us quite apart from the question of "happenedness." A detached analysis of historical detail can never be the only way into the text, nor ought one to wait for assured historical results before using the text for preaching and teaching purposes. Even where the historiographer's judgment may be negative in this regard, the material may still have much to say to the community of faith in any age. It is this conviction which underlies what we have to say in the following chapters.

Story and Structure

It has been suggested that anyone who studied Shakespeare's *Hamlet* with a view only to reconstructing the history of Denmark would be doing violence to that literary classic. At the same time, the Scriptures, and not least these historical books, are commonly studied primarily for the purposes of retrieving certain information from them, whether historical or theological. As a result they are commonly given a value which is commensurate with the amount or accuracy or sophistication of the information which they contain. In the two remaining sections, observations will be made regarding two approaches that do not have the collection of information from the text as a primary goal: literary and kerygmatic. Rather, the concern of these approaches is fundamentally a hearing of the text itself.

The new literary approach differs from prior studies primarily in its interest in literary criticism rather than literary history. That is to say, the basic concern is for texts as literary objects rather than for the history of the text prior to its present shape, or, for that matter, the historical context of the text. The assumption is that whatever sources may have been inherited, and used to give shape to the present text, the text makes sense in its present form apart from such knowledge. As a literary entity, it now has a life of its own and we need to come to terms with it as such. Thus, the amazing variety of literary features of the text may be examined to see how they work together to form an organic whole. While some scholars who take this approach might wish to dispense with historical considerations altogether, most would consider the literary and historical approaches to be complementary. Yet, as will be evident in the studies which follow, the literary approach is more fruitful than more narrow historical ones for getting inside a text, and seeing what really makes it tick.

Such an approach, long characteristic of the study of other literature, is in its infancy in biblical scholarship. While important studies of the deuteronomic history along these lines have begun to appear, they are relatively few in comparison to more historically oriented studies (see the works of Polzin and Gunn cited in the bibliography). It is clear, however, that students of the Scriptures will have to be increasingly attentive to this approach. To grapple with the way in which the Bible functions as literature will prove to be an important, indeed crucial, "handmaid" to any study of the Bible as Scripture, for it is in, and through, literary means that God has chosen to speak.

While there is some concern for pointing out literary features in each of the studies which follow, two more general literary considerations are in order at this point. The first has to do with the language of "story" to refer to biblical materials. The second attempts to lay out some of the literary structures evident in the deuteronomic history, in particular.

Story. As we have noted, the materials in Joshua–Kings are predominantly narrative in form. There is an occasional poetic piece (e.g., Judges 5), and some lists (e.g., Joshua 15), but the bulk of the material consists of a variety of narrative genres. It has become increasingly popular to use the general designation "story" for these narratives. That places the emphasis upon the imaginative character of the material and also focuses attention on the material from a literary perspective. But is it finally a satisfactory term?

One of the dangers is that the use of "story" might suggest (particularly to the popular mind) that we are dealing with material which is entirely imaginative and fictional, with no roots in what actually happened. However, in the preceding section we have noted that this literature does in fact reflect various aspects of the history of Israel. While not historiographical in character, with much imagination used in the telling, the material does have certain features associated with history-writing, e.g., the chronological framework, and its cumulative and developmental character. Moreover, a too-easy use of "story" could suggest that "happenedness" is totally unimportant for faith (cf. previous section). While "story" language may enable us to avoid certain unfruitful avenues of approach (e.g., that the value of the material is *necessarily* related to its "happenedness," or that God is revealed only in, and through, external events), it would be unfortunate if no distinctions were made between, say, the stories of Job, or Jonah, and the story of Israel in the deuteronomic history. The word "story" thus lacks the kind of precision we often need to have.

Another problem in the use of "story" is that it might suggest to many readers that the deuteronomic history is a unitary and original production like a modern novel. In reality it is a series of stories, originating in various times and places, finally put together in a kind of mosaic. And, while one does need to take very seriously the final form of the mosaic (as we do in the following chapters), recognition of the history of the literature gives one an important perspective on its nature. That is to say, one is thereby enabled to see the communal character of the literature; the deuteronomic history is finally a living, growing body of material, reflective of a variety of experiences in the life of the people of God (and of the life of God!) over a long period of time. Perhaps helpful analogies could be drawn at this point between it and Alex Haley's book, *Roots*.

Finally, and perhaps most importantly, "story" language does not sufficiently recognize the importance of generalizations in making sense of the biblical material. The analogy of a football game might be helpful here. One discerns what is involved, not simply by following the progress (the story) of a game, but by having available certain generalizations about the sport (on the basis of analyses, reflections, and argumentation about aspects of games already played). Only such generalizations, which are not reducible to story form, enable one to discern continuities, to know whether one is seeing something strange or radically new, and to realize when an objective has been reached.

Similarly, one might say that the deuteronomic editor provides just such generalizations at key junctures in the narrative (see examples in the discussion about structure below). These reflections, in effect, interrupt the flow of the story, or give internal directions as to how the story is to be read, rather than being integral to the story itself. The various stories in and of themselves may provoke all kinds of reactions in the reader, but the editorial reflections bring a suggested focus and make truth-claims, which decisively limit the number of possible interpretations. More generally, fundamental generalizations (often only alluded to here and there in the story) about God, about humans, about the world, about what good and evil are, etc., cut across all the stories and give to them not only a certain coherence but, as truth-claims, delimit possibilities of meaning. Thus, while the designation "story" enables us to avoid identification of this material with a theological treatise, nonetheless, theological generalizations, current in the story-telling community, have been incorporated into the stories and give them a certain decisive direction with respect to meaning. Nevertheless, if carefully qualified, and if more than literary considerations are allowed to control one's work with the material, the concept of "story" is a helpful entry point into the text.

Story is a very concrete and personal form of literature. As the Israelites told and retold the story, they were again and again drawn into it in such a way that it became their own story. As a result, they became participants in that great, yet often quite hidden, drama of divine action and human response. It was precisely at the juncture of past story and present reality that Israel came to know what it meant to be the people of God. Because there was a connection between one life-story and another, the faith was not merely an idea, but an embodiment, a way of life. The language and experience of faith thus remained concrete and personal.

Israel's story has the capacity of keeping the reader anchored in this world, rather than seeking to escape into an imaginary one. It does not dissolve into myth, into some mystical world of the gods which suppresses the human or the natural, or some religious world far removed from the secular sphere. By and large, the world reflected in these stories is ordinary, everyday, and familiar. It is filled with the surprises and joys, the sufferings and the troubles, the complexities and the ambiguities known to us all. At the same time, the story form allows for (in a way that history proper does not) an admixture of Israel's story and God's story. But even the latter component is seen to be this-worldly, as God works out purposes in the midst of a less than perfect world. And God's story has the ultimate purpose, not of bringing the people into some heavenly sphere, but of enabling a transformation of this life to emerge.

This capacity of the story to draw one into it in such a way as to encompass the full life of the reader means that the distance between past text/life-story, and present reader is overcome; the horizons merge. At the same time, readers will encounter aspects that are often quite different from their own stories: there are surprises, jolts, cold wind blasts, and discontinuities as past and present life-stories come into contact with one another. For some hearers, this may mean the rejection of the story. But, for those who respond positively, the story may provide a means for the shaping of identity (a constitutive function), or a mirror for self-identity (a descriptive function), or a model for the life of faith (a paradigmatic function). One may, thereby, not only come to be a member of the people of God, but also come to know who one is, and what shape the life of faith ought to take. Not just any story will accomplish these things. While stories generally have the capacity to affect people for good or ill, only God's involvement in Israel's story enables them to have an effect that is saving and blessing. Again, we see how certain truth-claims within the text move us beyond a simple literary approach to it.

Structure. There are two ways of developing this issue: we may attempt to find structures for the deuteronomic corpus as a whole, or use the present division into books as a basic framework. These approaches are not, necessarily, mutually exclusive; individual books may well be conceived of as "chapters" within the larger whole, and there may well be overarching structures which cut across those chapters. Both ways of structuring the history will be explored briefly here.

1. Overarching structures. This has been a key concern ever since Noth's pioneering work. It is clear that there is a unity of literary style and theological perspective throughout the history, though not present uniformly in all its sections. This "deuteronomic" perspective is present, in particular, in certain speeches and prayers spoken by leaders at key junctures in Israel's history, as well as in some transitional narratives. They are hortatory in character, and thus tend to look both to the past and to the future. Note that speeches by Joshua open and close the account of the conquest (chaps. 1 and 23); the period of the judges is introduced by a narrative (2:6–3:6), and closed by a speech of Samuel (1 Samuel 12); and the latter, in turn, prefaces the period of the monarchy. The transition from the early monarchy under Saul to the era of the Davidic covenant is marked by 2 Samuel 7: a speech by Nathan and a prayer by David. The Solomonic prayers in 1 Kings 8 punctuate the period of the United

Monarchy at the point of the building of the temple. The prophecy of Ahijah in 1 Kgs 11:29-39 serves to close the United Monarchy and open up the period of the divided kingdoms. The history of the North is closed with the narrative of 2 Kings 17, while the future of the South is sealed with the narrative of 2 Kings 21. The speech of Josiah in 2 Kings 23 serves to delay the announced fate of Judah, but in turn functions as a paradigm for Israel's future.

In addition, a number of shorter editorial comments, often evaluative in nature, are introduced throughout the narrative, particularly at transition points (e.g., between the stories of the judges and the kings). These provide additional clues to the concerns of the narrator(s).

2. Individual books. Brief notes regarding each of the four books may be helpful here, in order that the reader may grasp some of the basic concerns of the shorter units of the history, each of which has its own structure.

One striking structural element is that, after Joshua, every book begins with what would appear to be the end of a previous era, but by its placement it is made, rather, into the starting point for a new period (Judges 1; 1 Samuel 1ff.; 2 Samuel 1; 1 Kings 1–2; 2 Kings 1ff.).

The book of Joshua. The book is largely concerned with issues related to the settlement in the land of promise. It is framed by a prologue (chap. 1), and an epilogue (chaps. 22–24) that set out the specific agenda of the editor. (See the discussions of Joshua 1 and 24 below.) Chapter 1 begins with the central concerns that the land be seen as a gift, stresses the promise and presence of God, and continues with the importance of the human response in the face of what is to follow. Chapters 22–24 have in common a concern about the first commandment and the proper "service" of the Lord, especially in view of the fact that not all the indigenous peoples of the land have been driven out. The future of the people of God in the land will depend finally on whether they are able to "fear the Lord and serve him in sincerity and in faithfulness" (Josh 24:14). Yet, undergirding all of Israel's possibilities is the gracious action of God which has enabled Israel to come to this point in her life (24:2-13).

The body of the book (chaps. 2–21) serves to underline the latter point in a special way, though not without concern for faithful human response to God's activity. (See the discussion of Joshua 6 below.) Chapters 2–12 set forth the major aspects of the settlement, while chaps. 13–21, with their detail regarding the apportionment of the land to various tribes, serve to actualize the fulfillment of God's promise of land in a very concrete fashion.

The book of Judges. The book as a whole focuses on the "settling-in" period for Israel, an event which has a rippling effect on the rest of Israel's history. The prologue/epilogue format of Joshua is followed (see the structural observations in the discussion of Judges 2). The opening verses (1:1–2:5) provide a note of stability, while at the same time they introduce a matter which will prove to be Israel's eventual undoing: the nations with their idolatrous practices still survive in the land. The epilogue (chaps. 17–21) describes a very turbulent situation, and gives an indication of the disastrous effects that idolatry has had upon the community. It is striking that kingship is anticipated (21:25) as a possible way to meet problems, which have both political and religious aspects.

The heart of the book (3:6–16:31) consists of a series of stories about major and minor judges which God raised up for the salvation of Israel (there is an interpretive introduction in 2:6–3:6). Though it has been common to suggest that these stories show a recurrent pattern of human failure, divine anger, human repentance, and divine salvation, the discussion of 2:6–3:6 will show that there is no such simple schema. Rather, there is considerable variety both in human response and divine action, so that it would be preferable to use the image of a spiral: there are certain commonalities in the human failures in each generation, but the impact of the whole suggests a progressive intensification of apostasy.

The books of Samuel. While one might consider the period of judges to continue into the time of Samuel (cf. 1 Sam 7:15), the importance of the latter with respect to new prophetic and royal leadership means that he belongs more with the period which follows than with that which precedes.

The transitional passages at 1 Sam 13:1 and 2 Sam 1:1 would appear to break the material into three major divisions revolving around the key figures: Samuel (1 Samuel 1–12), Saul (1 Samuel 13–31), and David (2 Samuel). In terms of more general content, these divisions would mark the establishment, the failure, and the success of monarchical leadership. Framing the whole are two important poetical passages (1 Sam 2:1-10 and 2 Sam 22:1–23:7), which serve to lift up both the kingship of Yahweh and human kingship, the former providing the counterpoint for the latter throughout the narrative.

The importance of Samuel for all that follows cannot be stressed too much (see the discussion of 1 Samuel 3), especially for sorting out the different perspectives on kingship (1 Samuel 8–12), for the prophetic stance taken in the rejection of Saul, and for the election of David (1 Samuel 13–16). The rejection/election themes are then played out in 1 Samuel 17–31, with the death of Saul, and the establishment of the Davidic dynasty detailed in 2 Samuel 1–8 (see the discussion of 2 Samuel 7). The ark narratives in 1 Samuel 4–6 and 2 Samuel 6 provide the kingship of Yahweh counterpoint to these developments in Israel's kingship.

The "court history" (2 Samuel 9–20) focuses on critical events in the reign of David, not the least of which is the concern for whom his successor might be (on this narrative, and the important role of 2 Samuel 12, see the discussion below). As noted, the concluding chapters (21–24) provide some interpretive clues for an understanding of the kingship of David.

The books of Kings. Like the other books, 1 Kings begins with the end of an era, which now serves as the beginning of a new one. Thus the death of David is interwoven with the succession of Solomon in chaps. 1–2, while chaps. 3–11 focus on the reign of Solomon (with chap. 8 centering on the rule of God once again, in connection with the building of the temple). At the division of the kingdom, the narrator interweaves the histories of Israel and Judah in 1 Kings 12–2 Kings 17, the latter chapter marking the fall of the North. 2 Kings 18–25 concludes the corpus with the destruction of Jerusalem, the demise of the South, and the beginning of the Exile.

Interwoven throughout the books of Kings is the increasingly prominent role given to the word of God through the prophets. In fact, so prominent is their role considered to be, that in 1 Kings 17–2 Kings 9, we have more to do with the history of the prophets (particularly Elijah and Elisha) than with the kings (see below on 1 Kings 19 and 2 Kings 5). This serves to demonstrate that the word of God, both in grace and judgment, provides the perspective from which the history of Israel must finally be understood.

Message: What Issues Does It Address?

The deuteronomic history was written with a specific audience in view. The author(s) did not write for everybody in general or nobody in particular. This is less obvious in the case of narrative materials than it is, e.g., with the prophets, who commonly use second person pronouns to speak directly to their audience (e.g., Amos 4). Yet, there are a few texts in the history where the audience is explicitly in view (e.g., 1 Kgs 8:46-53). Such examples are sufficient to indicate that readers must be attentive to the specific audience to which these narratives were directed, and seek to discern what questions and issues of theirs were being addressed by these materials.

It might be objected that this material was intended for more than one audience. This follows from the observation that these books have undergone a complex history before reaching their present form. Thus, e.g., if the story of the ark (1 Samuel 4–6; 2 Samuel 6) originally existed as a separate narrative, distinct from its present context, then it was certainly intended to speak to a much earlier audience than the one intended in the final redaction. While it is certainly appropriate to give attention to earlier audiences who may have heard these stories along the way in Israel's history, the present volume limits itself to the audience to which the final edition was addressed, namely, the community of exiles in Babylon.

What do we mean when we use the word "message" to refer to these books? First of all, this means that the author had more than a literary, historical, or even theological focus. The hortatory style (exhortation) in some of the narratives indicates that they were used to address a community of faith. The overriding focus is on matters of fundamental concern to such a community, with judgment and promise being two of the more important ones. Given the hortatory style, the speaking from faith to faith, the dominant themes, and the fitness of these themes for an exilic situation, it is not surprising that these materials would have been heard as the Word of God.

There is a danger that emphasis upon "message" could lead to a search for some general religious truth or moral lesson in these texts. But that would be to misunderstand "message" and misuse such an approach. Message is not theology, though it is informed by a theological perspective. Message is a living, dynamic reality, always on the move with the people to whom it speaks, and cannot finally be reduced to a formula or dogmatic statement of truth. To speak of "message" means that the problems and possibilities of a particular community of faith are in view, and that the material has been shaped in such a way as to address those people with a Word of God. To resort to an old maxim, a word is being spoken, which is timely rather than timeless.

Moreover, to speak of "message" is not to limit the functioning of the material in a narrow way, as if it were designed to make a single point, in the sense of "the" message. There are several "interpenetrating visions" in this long narrative, but all such "visions" are capable of functioning for the community in such a way as to address its particular situation.

Another way of speaking about message is to say that it is always an "incarnate" word. That is to say, it comes to each audience clothed in human language. At the very least, this means that the message cannot be grasped apart from a thoroughgoing study of the language in which it is clothed. Because the Word of God is never pure, but always expressed and thus hidden in its human forms, the matter of understanding is always complex and remains incomplete and fragmented. It must always include rigorous historical and literary analysis, with the assumption that God has chosen to work through such human skills for the enhancement of understanding.

We would be naive to think that we can hear these narratives with the same clarity that the first hearers did. An equal naivete, however, would be to suggest that we have no access to their situation, or that it is irrelevant to know how the texts originally functioned. One way to proceed is to juxtapose narratives with issues faced by the people of God in the context to which the narratives were addressed. To lay contextual issues alongside narrative should enable illumination of the text, and give breadth and depth to the results of one's interpretation. This approach has the advantage of avoiding an abstract concern about what the author might have "intended." Rather, in the juxtaposition of context and text, we are concerned about what issues faced by the audience might have been addressed.

While it is simplistic to speak only of exilic questions to which the narratives bring "answers," this is, nonetheless, a helpful approach. In each of the studies below, one or more of the following concerns is assumed to exist among the exiles.

1. Questions of identity: Are we still the people of God, or has God abandoned us, perhaps forever?

2. Questions of guilt: What went wrong? Is all the blame to be placed on us? Is it possible for such heinous sins to be forgiven?

3. Questions of theodicy: Has God been fair to us? Does the punishment fit the crime? Were God's actions justified? Are we being punished for others' sins?

4. Questions of hope: Is there any basis for hope, or are we condemned to despair?

5. Questions of divine faithfulness: Will God remain true to the ancient promises? Do promises of land, prosperity, etc., still hold, or have they "gone by the boards"?

6. Questions of divine presence: With the destruction of the temple, is God present with the people anymore? Is God available where we now are?

7. Questions of divine power: Given Israel's defeat at the hands of enemies who served other gods, what does that say

about the power of Yahweh? Even if there is a will, has the deity ability to enact deliverance?

8. Questions of idolatry and syncretism: Has it paid us to worship only one God? Would it not serve our future better if we were more syncretistic?

9. Questions of purity: What should be our relationship to other peoples, given the troubles such mixing has occasioned for us in the past? Should we be separatistic?

10. Questions of continuity and change: To what extent, if at all, can we count on the old truths? Will long-standing symbols of the faith (e.g., the temple) remain a part of what it means to be the people of God?

11. Questions of beginning again: What ought to be the shape of the community on the other side of the Exile? What can we do to make sure that this does not happen again?

12. Questions of leadership: Given past patterns of leadership, what is appropriate for today and for whatever future God may have in store for us?

It would be a mistake to suggest that all the exiles were uniformly concerned with any or all of these questions. The literature which emerged from the Exile testifies not only to the variety of contextual issues, but also to the different ways of speaking to them. Second Isaiah, the Priestly writer, the deuteronomic historian, as well as others, have different ways in which they seek to speak to the issues of their contexts. At the least, however, one should keep these questions in mind as one reads the history, and thus the "fitness" of certain texts to certain questions will emerge in striking ways.

Although the Word of God is always addressed to a particular situation, the insights gained through hearing it will assist in the hearing of a Word in the contemporary situation. If the contemporary community of faith finds itself in a situation that is comparable to that of the text, a Word spoken back there and then may become a Word spoken here and now. Moreover, the specificity of analogous contexts may make the hearing even sharper. For example, the promises to the people of God in Josh 1:1-9, "God will not leave you or forsake you; he will not fail you" are words which may be taken to heart by the people of God in the present. They may become even more meaningful if the context is properly understood: a time when the community was looking into the teeth of a storm and a time of transition in leadership. Then, parallels may be drawn in terms of a comparable situation for the contemporary audience. When this specificity has been drawn out, the gospel word of the text has the capacity of striking home in ways that are not otherwise possible.

THE BOOK OF JOSHUA

A Word for a Time of Transition (Joshua 1:1-9)

● Though virtually all of the texts in the deuteronomic corpus had a history prior to their being incorporated into this larger body of material, these materials are finally used to address a very specific situation in the life of the people of God, namely, the exiles in Babylonia. Thus, we shall begin the study of some of the selected texts with concerns these exiles would have had, to provide a way of listening to the texts in a way in which the exiles would have listened to them (cf. pp. 46-47).

What has happened to the promises of God? The exiles have been driven away from the land promised to their fathers, with little or no hope of returning. Do these old promises still stand? However, it is not simply a question of God's promise: it is also a question of the divine presence. The temple, the place where God was thought to be truly present in the land, is now destroyed. Is God also present and active among the exiles, who wander among the nations far from home?

Is there anything that can be done about the future? The exiles are languishing under the heels of those who have destroyed all that they hold dear. They are certainly without power to do anything about their situation.

The leadership upon which Jerusalem had depended through the years had now been taken away. Will God raise up leaders for them once again? What kind of leaders ought they to be, and how should they be related to the rest of the people?

These opening verses of Joshua make clear the kind of "history book" we will encounter in Joshua through Kings. It is evident that the author is not setting out to reconstruct the history of Israel, beginning with the conquest. He does not introduce us to an annal of military exploits or give the data needed to reconstruct the history of the conquest or set an agenda for dealing with the broad sweep of Israel's history or indicate the sources and methods that he would use to give such a history. Rather, the book begins with a series of speeches by God (vv 1-9), Joshua (vv 10-15), and the people (vv 16-18). There is just enough narrative to give the speeches some coherence. Their content is such that one can only conclude that we have here a *theological* introduction to what follows. They focus on what God has done, or will do, and on what the appropriate response of the people ought to be.

> ● While literary and historical analysis will assist us in understanding these texts, and others which follow, the content makes it clear that only a thoroughgoing theological approach will enable the reader to have a proper understanding of them.

The story depicts very little in the way of military preparation; it is religious in character. The material in vv 1-9 is almost entirely an admixture of promises and exhortations; it is essentially sermonic, the importance of which we shall return to later. Suffice it to be said here that the initial part of the text consists largely of promises, whether recalling those spoken by God in the past (vv 3-4, 6), or to Joshua and his community in the present (vv 5-6). The promise to the fathers "surrounds" the latter (vv 3 and 6b). The remainder (vv 7-9) is largely hortatory in character. This is anticipated in v 6a: "Be strong and of good courage," and this theme surrounds the next section (v 7*a* and v 9*a*). Verse 9*b* then returns to the element of promise, being essentially repetitive of the key element in v 5. The passage may be outlined as follows:

1. Transition and introduction (vv 1-2).
2. Promise (vv 3-6), with anticipatory hortatory element (v 6*a*).
3. Exhortation (vv 7-9), with recollective promise element (v 9*b*).

The centrality of the promise in the author's thought is evident in the fact that it is included in the introduction of God's address to Joshua (v 2) and that it closes off the speech of God (v 9*b*). The promise thus "surrounds" the law and the exhortation to obedience; it provides the center for interpretation. Moreover, the fact that they are presented in this order indicates an intended theological relationship between promise and exhortation, a matter to which we will return.

- This demonstrates the importance of literary analysis in getting at the central concerns of the text.

The fact that we are dealing with a deuteronomic author/editor is clear from the fact that the section consists entirely of a patch-work of expressions from Moses' speeches in Deuteronomy. Verse 2 corresponds to Deut 10:11, and thus stresses the continuity of leadership. Verses 3-5*a*, a virtual quotation of Deut 11:24-25, serves the function of stressing that God is faithful to promises and that the time for their fulfillment is now at hand. Verses 5*b*-7*a*, largely repeating Deut 31:6-8, 23, indicate God's reaffirmation of the promises and exhortations at the point of transition in leadership (they also serve to enhance the authority of Joshua). Verses 7*b*-8 are reminiscent of a series of texts in Deuteronomy which identify the latter with the "book of the law" and stress the importance of meditation and obedience (see Deut 5:32-33; 17:18-19; 30:10).

Key elements of Deuteronomy are thus pulled together and become foundation pieces for understanding the materials which follow. It is as if the author is saying: If you want to understand properly the story which follows, you must read it within the theological context provided by the book of Deuteronomy.

We should now move to a brief consideration of the relationship of this introduction to the materials which follow in Joshua. The remainder of the book of Joshua may be divided into two basic parts: the settlement in the land of Canaan (chaps. 2–12) and the distribution of that land among the tribes (chaps. 13–23). Joshua provides the leadership for both tasks, tasks which serve to coordinate the fulfillment of God's promises. Two questions arise: How faithful is God to his promises? How faithful is Joshua in carrying out the tasks given him by God?

With regard to the latter question, it becomes clear that Joshua does well, and is recognized for it (see 3:7, 4:14, 6:27). Yet, it is also clear that Joshua does not adhere to the admonition of 1:7, to turn not from the law "to the right hand or to the left." Our discussion of chap. 6 will enable us to pursue this matter further.

As for the former question, there is some ambivalence in the texts. On the one hand, there are strong affirmations that the entire land has been taken (see 11:23, 21:43-45, 23:14); on the other hand, there are indications that territory remains to be taken (13:1, 6-7; 15:53; 23:4-13). Is it possible to reconcile these notices? The detailed descriptions in Joshua (and Judges 1) conform to the latter perspective; the former are found only in summary statements. These statements have commonly been interpreted as idealized or exaggerated or even ironic. Each of those directions has merit, but it is possible that the statements are nothing more than theological judgments, intending to make clear that God's promises have been fulfilled. That seems to be the force of 21:43-45, and 23:14 in particular. The use of the language of fulfillment, of course, does not entail literal fulfillment. All of the promises did come to pass, not with the kind of a precision that a biblical fundamentalist might like to see, but a decisive fulfillment nonetheless. The fulfillment is decisive enough that an allotment of the not-yet-conquered territory can occur (13:6-7, 23:4); they have gained essential control of the land, though without eliminating all opposition. A fulfillment does not suggest that there is no work yet to be done (23:5ff.); God and people are faced with a continuing task, though the basic struggle is over. The themes of decisive fulfillment and continuing task are joined in Joshua 23 (cf. 23:14 with 23:13, 4, 7), and this suggests a general direction for interpretation (see also Deut 7:22; 19:8-9). Such tension provides a vehicle for the author to emphasize the need of obedience, and yet to affirm the gift of fulfillment.

● One of the difficulties in interpreting these passages may be an all-too-easy assumption that the biblical authors were literalists in their understanding of the fulfillment of God's promises. It is clear that prophecy and fulfillment are important for the author, and that he understands that the history of Israel is made possible because the word of God is at work in it. But, any understanding of fulfillment must recognize that God does not work independently from what human beings are doing. There is a constant interaction between divine Word (Promise) and human response, and to such a degree that the latter can affect the shape of the fulfillment of the former (cf. Josh 23:5 with 23:15-16).

Nevertheless, there is some remaining tension in the book which cannot be smoothed over. The interpreter needs to be careful not to harmonize what may be an intended tension. In any case, the explication of the message is not finally dependent upon an assured historical reconstruction of the history of the period in question.

The key theological emphases, and the force this passage had for the author's contemporaries in exile, now need attention.

The most predominant theme, seen in the literary structure as well as in the dominance of a certain vocabulary, is that the land is God's gift to Israel, a gift which is the fulfillment of promises to the patriarchs and to Moses. That theme of promise and gift is found nine times in the opening chapter (vv 2, 3, 4, 6, 11, 13, 14, 15, 16).

This may well lead to another understanding of the tension we have seen between theological statement and historical reality. Israel did not deserve either promise or gift. Great pains are taken in Deut 9:5ff. to point out that Israel did not receive the land "because of your righteousness." In fact, much of

Deuteronomy 9 suggests even more, namely, that Israel deserved destruction rather than land. Israel has escaped the merited judgment of God solely because of the unmerited mercy of God (see Deut 10:10-11). Thus, a strong statement about the fulfillment of the promise would now serve to emphasize the extraordinary mercy which God has visited upon the people. The land is not only a gift, it is a merciful gift.

Another factor relating to the land as gift is brought out by the language indicating that the land has *already* been given to them (v 3). The land is theirs for the taking; God has delivered it into their hands and is the one who has achieved the victory (cf. 23:10, 13). Thus, the settling in the land can only be viewed as appropriation (or possession, v 11; cf. Deut 1:8, 39), not as achievement (cf. Josh 24:13; Deut 8:17-18, 6:10-11). The land is not only unmerited, it is not "worked for." In addition, the continued use of the participle for "give" (vv 2, 11, 15; cf. Deut 1:20, 25 and throughout) indicates more than an initial giving: God *continues* to give the land to the people. It is never finally theirs to possess without the giver. And the gift of land is the gift of salvation, salvation being understood fundamentally as a life of well-being.

The theme of the gift of the land is integrally related to the theme of promise, as we have seen. The promise had been given to the fathers, Abraham, Isaac, and Jacob (v 6), and reiterated to Moses (v 3), and it is that promise which is about to be fulfilled. Israel's continued life is thus dependent upon the promise; the promise is constitutive for Israel's existence. This promise is not something which has been spoken one time in the past and then "forgotten," that is, ceased to be heard along the way in Israel's life only finally to "show up" at the time of fulfillment. As the text makes clear, it was given again and again. The word of promise is thus constantly at work, giving shape to Israel's life. God has been the continuity in Israel's story, enabling it to arrive at this historic juncture.

But, it is not only the promise of the land which is central to this text. There is also the promise of continuing divine care and presence. God will be with Joshua and, hence, with the people (vv 5, 9; cf. Deut 31:8 with 31:6). God is not confined to some locale, such as the ark of the covenant (or the temple!), but rather is "with you wherever you go" (v 9). God will not "fail you" (v 5) (lit., "let you drop or sink down"); the image is that of a God who holds the people in his hands and will not let them go (cf. Josh 10:6; Jer 38:4). In every case in the OT where this language is used (e.g., Jer 1:8; Isa 43:5), it is expressive of God's graciousness, in which the people are called to trust, and which makes faithfulness possible.

Now, it is precisely this element of promise that is crucial to an understanding of the remainder of the text. The promise precedes the word of exhortation: "Be strong and of good courage (or, remain firm, resolute)." This is essentially a call to faithfulness, and not a formula of encouragement (cf. v 9*a,* where this is understood as a command, and vv 7, 18, where "only" is used). It is not a word which calls Joshua to pull himself up by his own bootstraps, as if by some sheer strength of personal will he can remain firm in the face of the tasks that lie ahead. The prior word of promise provides an essential context for, and indeed the basis of, the exhortation, and it is that word which finally enables such a response from Joshua (cf. Josh 10:25; Hag 2:4-5). God will be with him in everything, and without that no meaningful future is possible, no matter what strength of will is applied. Joshua is only called to be faithful and trusting. He does not have to be strong and firm so that God will not fail or leave him; God will not fail, come what may.

This word of promise also stands prior to the call to be obedient to the law (vv 7-8). The call to faithfulness is repeated in v 7*a,* this time with an explicit indication of the way in which such faithfulness can be manifested in life. Joshua's relationship with God is, of course, already presupposed in these verses; it is not something that needs to be established. Thus, the question of obedience to the law is not some legalism by which the relationship is to be established. It is concerned only with answering the question: What shape should the life with God, the life of faith, take? Given the relationship, how can life be shaped to be commensurate with that relationship? One basic way in which faithfulness is manifested is through obedience to the Torah ("law"). "By this book of the Torah," the author means essentially the book of Deuteronomy (though, within the final shape of the canon, it has reference to the entire Pentateuch). In either case, it refers to more than the "legal" sections of the Torah; it includes both promise and law.

● The "book" status of the Torah, and the admonition to meditate on it unceasingly and adhere to its concerns unstintingly, ought not suggest a religious rigidity or some early "Bible Belt" mentality. Its book status can be understood in a quite "evangelical" manner, functioning not unlike the Scriptures for many modern Jews and Christians. The uncompromising concern for attentiveness to its every detail has a fundamentally gracious intention, for through it God has provided a way of life that is in Israel's best interests.

But problems with these verses remain. Is the conquest of the land made conditional upon obedience? No such implication seems to be drawn here; no connection is made between the land and obedience, or land and success, or land and prosperity (cf. Deut 11:22-23, where at an earlier stage the language is more explicit). Moreover, there is no statement regarding the negative effect of *disobedience,* so common to Deuteronomy (e.g., 8:19-20), and occurring later in Joshua (23:15-16). This would appear to be a more general reference to success in Joshua's undertakings (see Deut 29:9; 30:9-10, 16). It needs to be remembered that this is a word to Joshua, and not a word to the whole people of God. It is a matter of Joshua's faithfulness, evidenced in a life of obedience, that will make a difference regarding *his* success. The possession of the land by the people of God is not made dependent upon Joshua's faithfulness alone; theoretically, another leader could be chosen.

Moreover, it is clear from what follows, particularly in the story of Achan, that there is disobedience among the people. *Nevertheless,* they are given the land. This indicates that any talk of "conditionality" in this chapter is really not in order. Not only is the law allowed to be interpreted in the light of the situation (see below on chap. 6), but even when disobedience occurs, the promise remains at work. Deut 9:6 comes into play here—it is not because of any righteousness or perfect obedience on the people's part that enables the possession of the land. As Deut 9:7ff. makes clear, God could well have followed through with judgment because of disobedience, but patience finally prevails over wrath. Moreover, as in the story of Achan, disobedience at the individual level does not place the entire community under judgment. The promise remains intact in the face of disobedience. Yet, there is a limit to divine patience, and at this point Joshua 23, and Israel's *continued* life on the land, comes into play.

There is still another problem here. How is it that the text can make such an easy correlation between obedience to the law and success and prosperity? It is a common theme in the deuteronomic literature that obedience will lead to life and blessing (see Deut 30:9-10, 16): be attentive to the shape of the life of faith, and benefits will follow. It simply follows from a certain type of life that things will go well, not always, of course, in some mechanical sort of way, but generally speaking. Normally, a life of obedience to the law, which was given out of God's concern for the best interests of the people, will lead to the good life in the good land. And because, for the deuteronomist, the commandments are understood as theoretically keepable (see Deut 30:11-14), it seems entirely reasonable to suggest that from obedience will issue the good life.

Moreover, success is not to be understood as a reward. It is not that God, in some forensic act, determines in connection with every obedient action that such positive effects will follow from it. Rather, God has established an order to life, so that good normally will intrinsically follow from obedience; that is a part of the moral order of things. But, even though God does not act directly in bringing it about, success is finally a gift, too, for it is enabled by a continuing providential work in the world. It is a blessing.

> • In this day of ecological sensitivity one might see this principle at work in a passage like Deut 22:6-7: If one is concerned about birds, that will indeed be a positive effect upon human life.

The other major theme in this material might be called a theology of leadership (or ministry).

First of all, the important place that Moses has in the chapter needs to be noted (he is mentioned eleven times!). Moses is called the servant of the Lord, again and again (1, 2, 7, 13, 15). He is recognized for his role as mediator of the divine promises (vv 3, 13), of the law (v 7), and of instructions for possessing the land (v 13, where the single quotation marks in RSV should extend through v 15; cf. Deut 3:18-20). He is one with whom God was especially present (vv 5, 17). And, most remarkable of all, to him is ascribed the gift of the land beyond the Jordan (vv 14, 15; cf. 13:8), and the obedience of the people (v 17).

Joshua assumes each of Moses' roles, though Moses remains the primary figure (see 11:15). He is the servant of the Lord (24:29); he mediates the divine promises, law, and instructions (vv 11, 12-15; cf. 22:1-6); God is with him in a special way (v 5, 17; cf. 3:7); he gives the land to the people ("causes to inherit" in v 5; see 11:23); receives their obedient response (1:16-17), and even more (4:14).

A most significant role is given to the human leader of the people of God. For all practical purposes, Moses and his successor can be said to stand before the people in the place of God. Thus, God wins the victory for the people, but works in important ways through those who are called to be leaders, and makes sure that there is a succession of such persons in leadership positions.

● One might call attention to other such successions in the deuteronomic history, cf. 1 Kgs 2:2-4; 2 Kgs 2:1 ff., and beyond that to NT understandings of apostleship.

It should be noted that, while God's *gift* is certain, human faithfulness is called for. This is not an unimportant consideration, else no attention would be given to the matter. Moreover, while the achievement of victory is finally God's, the proper appropriation of its effects is integral to life on the new land (hence, there is lengthy concern with allotment in chaps. 13–22).

Again, the human element is not left without importance in a context so filled with the mighty deeds of God.

Finally, attention should be directed to the kerygmatic use of these materials. The author makes use of these old traditions to speak a word of God to his contemporaries. The parallels between past and present are striking. The exiles, too, are a people who stand outside of the promised land, but who have a promise from God that the land, now under foreign domination, has been given to them. Even the total collapse of the nation and the death of key leaders (like Moses!) could not make null and void these divine promises.

The exiles are like the wandering Israelites in another way. They are totally without power to bring about their (re)entry into the land. They are dependent upon God for the next stage of their life; any victory will be the deity's, not theirs. They can only hear the word of promise and trust it. To live by the promise involves risk and vulnerability, for it may appear insubstantial in the face of a land full of "Canaanites." It would be safer to accept the situation as it is, as many exiles eventually did. But, the promise calls the people to a new future. The call is to be faithful to the God who gives the promise, and to trust that the future contains more "promise" than the present.

But it is not only the promise of the land that is important for the exiles. The question of the presence of God outside the promised land had become an issue for these displaced persons (cf. Lam 5:20-22). One strong affirmation of these verses is the continuity with regard to the divine presence. As God was with Moses, so he would be with Joshua and his people. Just as God's presence continued from the wandering period of Israel's life to the settled period, so also could the exiled community count on such continuity in the transition from this new time of wandering to the return to settlement in the land. As it once was, so it will be again.

Moreover, the human response of faithfulness is still important. The exiles are to be strong and remain firm in their faith, to trust in the God of the promise. One fundamental way in which this faithfulness can show itself in daily life is through continued attentiveness to Torah. In it God has provided a shape for life that is in Israel's best interests, that will enable blessing: the good life on the good land, once again. Moreover, there may be the suggestion that the exiles are to be responsive to their leaders as Israel once was (1:16-18). There may even have been concern among the exiles regarding the proper succession of human leadership. A proper way is outlined, unlike the one characteristic of kings in Israel's later life.

The sermonic character of these materials, then, makes it clear that they are not recorded out of some antiquarian interest. Rather, they provide a word of hope for the exiles; God is faithful to promises and remains eager to grant Israel rest (1:13) in the land. Yet, human faithfulness is crucial if future Israel is to avoid the failures so characteristic of her past.

• This text will function in particular during times of transition in the life of the community of faith. It is a text for any time at the boundary. As such, the key emphases in the kerygmatic section become available to the preacher. In the midst of whatever fears or uncertainties abound in "boundary times," questions regarding the promises and presence of God can be answered with the gospel affirmations repeated throughout this text: God will not leave you or forsake you; God will not fail you; God will be with you wherever you go.

It is precisely these *promises* that need to be lifted up and emphasized, in the face of the inevitable temptation to put the stress upon obedience to the law, or on success and prosperity. The call in the text is to be faithful in the midst of the fears and uncertainties, a faithfulness that is finally possible because the promises of God are at work in people's lives. The concern for constant attentiveness to the book of the law is not legalism; the concern is fundamentally gracious, for these "Scriptures" are God-given resources for life. Moreover, the reference to success and prosperity is not a *call* to be successful. It is another promise of God. Success will come, but not in a simplistic way; success lies on the far side of a tremendous battle. And it is, finally, only because God is at work in all of the undertakings of the people, that good results will be forthcoming. It is not at all clear what those good results will be, and they may not be what the people want or expect.

Yet, because God is at work, there will be good results. Success, finally, is a gift of God. At the same time, human faithfulness is not unimportant. Faithfulness will make a difference in what happens: it will make a difference for God (who has chosen to work through people), and it will make a difference for the world.

God and War (Joshua 6:1-27)

"And the walls came a 'tumblin' down." Joshua and the battle of Jericho is a story familiar to many, whether from Sunday school days, the Negro spiritual, or some Cecil B. DeMille extravaganza. Yet, for all its familiarity, it presents a number of problems for the contemporary interpreter, problems which also happen to be related to issues central to the thought of the deuteronomic historian.

We begin by noting how this material might have addressed the people in exile. What questions might they have had to which this narrative could have been a response?

The prophets in their midst kept speaking of the promises of God, assuring them that they had not been forgotten, and that they would once again be restored to their land (see Ezek 37:1-14). How could that be possible, given their state of powerlessness? They certainly did not have the military resources necessary to mount an attack against those who held their land. What possible role could they play to bring about the fulfillment of such promises? Moreover, given what had happened to them and their land, they may also have questioned whether their God had the power to enable such a return. Might not the deity also be powerless, in the face of such military might as held their land in thrall?

In addition, should they be returned to their land, what role would its present inhabitants play in that future? It seemed clear that mixing with the inhabitants of the land at the religious level had been one of the key factors that led to the Exile. How ought they to relate to those who possessed the land now? Ought the ancient ban be introduced upon any return, so that all possible intermixture with "heretics" would be eliminated? Or, was the issue more complicated than that? Were there people in the land who might not only assist them in any return, but should be integrated into the promised new community?

Numerous attempts have been made to trace the origins of the material in Joshua 1–12, none of which has achieved a consensus among scholars. Efforts to track the Pentateuchal traditions (J, E, P) through Joshua have largely been given up, though traces may be evident (e.g., E in Joshua 24). Generally, most scholars would say that these chapters contain a variety of stories relating to Israel's initial entry into the land, most of which had connections originally primarily with Benjaminite territory. These were collected at some point, given an all-Israel orientation, and finally shaped by the deuteronomic historian.

In many ways Joshua 6 is the center of this longer narrative in Joshua 1–12. All the key themes may be found here: land as gift of God; God as Warrior; the leadership of Joshua; the obedient response of the people; the use of various elements of Yahweh war, including the ban (see below); and the success. It might be said that the chapter functions as a prototypical conquest, and thus serves as a paradigm in the light of which all the conquest materials are to be interpreted. Joshua 24:11 (see 2:1-12) is evidence that the entire conquest could be spoken of in terms of what happened at Jericho.

The way in which the story is told would also seem to demonstrate its centrality, and may also give us some indication of the roots of the tradition. The story is told in terms of a religious ceremony. It is striking, the degree to which, in a larger narrative dealing with the conquest of the land, the warlike elements are here so subdued (note that Josh 24:11 indicates that the story *could* have been told in other terms). Verses 3-16 in particular suggest more the festive mood of a celebration than preparation for an actual battle. The presence of so many religious leaders, the precise arrangement of the people, officials, and ark, as well as the careful procedures regarding who, when, and where, would seem to betray the markings of a long-standing ritual (see Ps 48:12). On the other hand, the climax of the story—the falling of the wall—is reported in only one brief statement (v 20b).

Literary features suggest this as well. While there is a clear story line through the chapter, it is not a very straightforward one. It is filled with repetition, digression, and apparent inconsistencies. Directions for taking the city are given by God to Joshua (vv 2-5), interpreted by Joshua to the priests (v 6) and people (vv 7, 10), and finally described (vv 8-9, 11-21). A digression seems to be present in vv 17-19. Verbal repetitions are common: marching around the city (7 times); the number seven (14 times); the ark (9 times); trumpets, ram's horns (19 times); the shout (7 times); and priests (9 times).

For these reasons, then, some scholars contend that this chapter reflects liturgy that was regularly used to celebrate the conquest of the land, in conjunction with a ceremony celebrating the Jordan crossing (Joshua 3–4 also bears many liturgical characteristics; cf. chap. 24). The narrator would thus have used existing liturgical materials in telling the story. While the existence of such a ritual cannot be proved, the casting of the story in such terms demonstrates that it was intended to be understood as one would a liturgy. That is to say, it is to be understood typologically (or mythologically) as a constitutive event in terms of which Israel is continually to understand itself.

● Note how analysis of the language alone, apart from any certain knowledge of the history of this tradition, enables proper interpretation. This demonstrates that literary analysis must always accompany historical analysis. At the same time, literary analysis points beyond itself to a very important situation in Israel's life.

The language used also enables us better to understand the question of the relationship of this text to historical reality. Archaeologists have traced the history of Jericho in the 2nd millennium B.C., and have shown beyond a reasonable doubt that Jericho was at best a small military outpost at the time of the Israelite settlement in the land (13th cent.). The walls of Jericho have indeed collapsed, but the destruction is dated prior to 1550, well before Israel's entry into the land under Joshua.

This need cause neither despair nor cynicism. The evidence

suggests, not that the story was exaggerated over the years, but that as a consequence of telling and retelling, stories about the main Israelite entry and ones about previous entries through Jericho (perhaps by tribal groups that later became a part of Israel, and whose story became the story of all Israel) became merged with one another. Whatever the author's knowledge of the actual event may or may not have been, he shapes the story in liturgical terms, and thereby indicates that he has no interest in some reconstruction of "what actually happened at Jericho," but rather intends to drive home the meaning of the conquest for the faith and life of the people of God.

   • Given the ritualized language it is impossible to reconstruct what actually occurred at Jericho. It has been suggested that an earthquake was responsible for laying the walls flat. It may well be that the trumpet blasts were intended to simulate the quaking, as they almost certainly do in Exod 19:18-19 (a narrative also shaped by liturgical practice, cf. also Exod 14:21-22). While such may have been the understanding of those who heard this story, this does not suggest simply a natural explanation would have been given for what occurred. It is God's action that has made the taking of the city possible (see vv 2, 16), whether working through an earthquake or just the ritual activity of the people.

What is the intended meaning? The primary focus is to emphasize that the promised land is a *gift* of God. The land has been given to the people (vv 2, 16); it is theirs for the taking. The immediately preceding narrative (5:13-15), depicting an appearance of "the commander of the army of the Lord" to Joshua "by Jericho," is certainly intended to suggest that what follows is due to the activity of God. (See Exod 3:4-5 for a comparable introduction to what occurs in Egypt and at the Red Sea.) And, as we have seen in our discussion of chap. 1, the land is given by God in fulfillment of promises to Moses and the fathers (1:3, 6). God is a promise-keeper.

So much has the action of God prepared the way for the taking of the city that Israel is depicted as meeting with no resistance at all. Not so much as a "shot" is fired by the other side! The victory is God's. After the walls fall down and open up the city, the Israelites just go in and mop up (6:20-21). They have been constituted as a people in the land because of what God has promised and accomplished, and not because of who they are or what they have done.

● One of the striking things about this story is the widely different ways in which moderns have responded to it. On the one hand, the story has captured the imagination of the people of God: witness the Negro spiritual and the common use of the story in Sunday school lessons. Particularly for those who are powerless (the blacks, children), it has served as a powerful symbol of hope and God's care for the powerless community. On the other hand, it has been viewed as naive, impossible, and even brutal by many, including members of the community of faith. Such attitudes arise largely because of certain presuppositions, both historical and theological. Historically, it is difficult to deal with the understanding of cause and effect, which this text reflects. Theologically, it is hard to imagine God's involvement in such an affair, let alone issuing commands for a bloodbath. While such problems must not be dismissed in a cavalier way, the alternative perspective suggested above is certainly in essential continuity with the fundamental import that the text had for ancient Israel.

This is a demonstration of the complexities of the hermeneutical task. The life situation and presuppositions of the reader profoundly affect the way in which the text is interpreted. For one group, the text is immediately appropriable because of continuities between ancient and modern life situations. For other people, a whole variety of questions need to be dealt with (see below) before any appropriation of the text can take place.

It would be a mistake to suggest that the response of the people is irrelevant. While the land is a gift and it is possible for Israel to possess it only because of God's victory, human activity plays an important, and indeed indispensable, role (cf. Judg 5:23). This is true in a number of ways:

a) It was possible for the people to reject the gift, to be unfaithful to the God of the promise, and hence not participate in its fulfillment. Thus, death is seen as a possibility for individuals who "rebel against your (Joshua's!) commandment and disobey your words" (1:18). This in fact happens in 7:24-25, and because of the "orders" given by Joshua it was potentially possible at Jericho. This seems to be the reason for at least some of the repetition in the story, as in v 8, where the people are noted as being obedient to the word of Joshua. So also v 20*a,* which could be understood as confusing the sequence of events between vv 16 and 20*b,* would seem to function only as a general statement highlighting the obedient response to Joshua's command (translate v 20*a:* "And so the people shouted *when* the trumpets were blown").

The "gift" word to Joshua in vv 2-5 places certain obligations upon the people. They are minimal when one considers the magnitude of the task, yet there is no indication that the taking of the city would have been possible without the actions of the community. God chooses to be dependent upon people in carrying out tasks in the world. The level of their participation is such, however, that they can only laud God's victory and not their own activity related thereto.

b) The leadership of Joshua is significant here, and he is given recognition for it (6:27; cf. 4:14). This is especially striking at two points: In the first place, when given directions by God for the taking of the city (vv 2-5), he then *interprets* this to two groups (priests, v 6; people, vv 7, 10, 16-19). It is noteworthy that he does not simply repeat the words of the Lord to them; he adds some of his own touches. He adds directions about the placement of the armed men (v 7), the silence of the people (v 10), and introduces his own command into the sequence of trumpet and shout (vv 10, 16).

● Thus, Joshua, as with all of God's chosen leaders in the OT, is not a "typewriter" in the hands of God. His task is to interpret the word of God that he has received in the light of his own assessment of the situation.

This understanding of the relationship between God's words and Joshua's interpretation removes some of the reasons commonly cited for separating the chapter into distinct sources; they need not represent inconsistencies.

Second, Joshua not only adds a word about the ban (vv 17-19), but makes a significant exception to it (Rahab's family). This is striking, not only because God has made no reference to such exception, but also because such an exception stands at odds with God's directive to him in 1:7, "being careful to do according to all the law which Moses my servant commanded you; turn not from it to the right hand or to the left." Because Moses' words in Deut 20:16 stated clearly that "you shall save alive nothing that breathes" in the war against the Canaanite cities, Joshua would appear to be disobedient to Moses' words (cf. also Joshua 9). But, rather than view it as disobedience, one ought to understand that the leadership of Joshua is given such stature that in the light of the circumstances, viz., the help given by Rahab to Israel and the promise extended to her, her family ought to be made an exception to the ban (see v 27). This is especially striking in view of the fact that Achan was executed because of his failure to adhere to the ban (chap. 7, cf. 1 Samuel 15).

● These exceptions point to the fact that context was considered crucial in any interpretation of the Torah. We are not informed what it is about the context that occasions the allowance of exceptions, but the freedom in interpretation is remarkable. And this freedom is understood in such a way that, even with the exceptions Joshua makes, he can be said to have fulfilled all of the commands (see 11:15!).

c) The role of Rahab, the non-Israelite prostitute, in the story is another testimony to the importance of human action in the conquest of the land. It is twice affirmed (vv 17, 25) that her family was saved because of her hiding of the Israelite messengers (see chap. 2), and because a promise had been made (v 22; cf. 2:14). Thus, an act of treason is seen to be integral to the success of the venture. A whole range of human action, even treasonous harlots, are used to accomplish God's purposes.

● Such human involvement in a story so filled with divine activity
significantly qualifies any suggestion that God is in "control" of
this, or other such events. The story could have turned out quite
differently if the human beings involved had chosen to take other
forms of action.

The other side of the Rahab story is the salvation that comes to
a group of non-Israelites who are in no way deserving. The story
is more than an etiological explanation of why the family of
Rahab was found among the Israelites (see 6:25). It serves to
qualify any notion that Israel may have had that its unique status
when compared to other peoples was deserved. This point is also
evident in Joshua 9, where the Gibeonites, too, are saved from
the ban and allowed to be a part of life in the new land (cf. 8:33,
35). Just as Israel experienced deliverance because of a promise,
and not because of any merit, for she was a stubborn people (see
Deut 9:4-5), so also Rahab was the recipient of a promise and
receives life thereby.

● Thus the story of Rahab reinforces the theme of the priority of
grace in God's dealings, not only with the chosen people, but with
all creatures. Moreover, while God's focus is on Israel, it is not
exclusively Israel-oriented. A larger purpose for all creatures
becomes evident in this account.

We must now deal with that most difficult aspect of this and
other chapters in Joshua, namely, the ban element of the "holy
wars" waged by Israel (chaps. 6, 8, 10, 11). Deuteronomy 20:16f.
states the matter succinctly: "But in the cities of these peoples
that the Lord your God gives you for an inheritance, you shall
save alive nothing that breathes, but you shall utterly destroy
them" (cf. Deut 7:2).

● We need to recognize how much our modern, western, and
commonly liberal frame of reference makes for difficulties in
handling these texts. Our perspective on matters of religious
tolerance is generally quite liberal, and we have not only learned to
live with religious pluralism, even some of the more kooky brands,

but have embraced it (though a Jonestown now and then brings us up short!). And, while we are normally not thoroughgoing pacifists, but espouse some form of "just war" theory, the deliberate killing of women and children turns our stomachs. All the canons of human justice are violated. And we get even more uncomfortable when we see texts like this misused to justify modern "holy wars" of various sorts. But, it is perhaps our theological convictions that occasion the greatest difficulties. A perceived theological sophistication leads us to object to the idea that this God, whom we define largely in terms of love and mercy, could be associated with (or even command!) such violence. Or, even more seriously perhaps, we believe in a sovereign God who controls the direction of history, and hence find ourselves in an inherent contradiction when we try to suggest that God is in no way responsible for such happenings as Jericho. Some new directions in our theology are necessary at both of these points.

In dealing with this subject, we need to eliminate attempts to escape from the hard realities with which these texts deal.

a) "These wars were simply defensive wars." Joshua 6 and other texts clearly indicate the offensive nature of at least some of Israel's undertakings, however.

b) "These wars did not actually occur or only rarely so." It may well be that the possession of the land was a more peaceful process than Joshua suggests (see Judg 2:23), but it is likely that some such activity occurred, and, in any case, the texts represent Israel as engaging in such wars. See Josh 6:21, 24, where every human being is killed and then burned with fire. Thus, the problem remains.

c) "These wars did occur, but texts such as Joshua 6 are not to be taken at face value; the author has purposely overdrawn what Israel actually did in order to make a point. Written in the light of the negative influence that Canaanite idolatrous practices had on Israel through the centuries (see 2 Kings 17), the author's retrospective vision is that this sort of decimation is what Israel ought to have done. Thus, these texts would have had a symbolic value for their audience, stressing the importance of separateness from such idolatrous peoples, rather than being a literal description of something which actually occurred." Again, while we might grant that some idealization has occurred for the sake of symbolic value, the matter is presented in such a variety of types of language and literature that it is difficult to consider all of it as symbolic. But, even to use such symbolic language to make a point, or to suggest that this is what Israel ought to have done, leaves the problem unresolved.

d) "These wars did occur in *early* Israel, but lessened in severity as the years went by. Note that the later actions of David (2 Samuel 8) are strong, but tempered when compared to those of Joshua. And, even Deuteronomy 20 makes a distinction between killing inhabitants of Canaan and all other nations with whom Israel might go to war. One could thus say that those earliest wars against the Canaanites were of a special sort, and hence the matter of the destruction of all human life did not apply later to other peoples." However, one may also point to such passages as Isa 63:1-6, or to such "reverse holy wars" where Israel is the object (cf. Deuteronomy 28), and see that wholesale human destruction remained a part of Israel's thinking when it reflected on divine judgment.

e) "A distinction needs to be made between OT and NT realities. There is a movement from an OT God who *uses* violence in achieving purposes, to a NT God who *absorbs* violence in achieving them." This is almost certainly an inadequate perception, since both modes of action are attested in each testament. Much of the difference in tone can be ascribed to the fact that the NT community of faith is not a state and does not aspire thereto. The God of the OT is certainly a God who absorbs much violence (as we shall see), and the God of the NT uses violence in ways that are actually much more severe than those found in the OT. A God who consigns the wicked to weeping and gnashing of teeth in the fires of hell for an eternity exercises a level of violence nowhere to be found in the OT.

f) An escape of a different order, but still an escape, is to attribute the "ban" to the mysterious ways of God, and then to suggest that any attempt to justify *God's* actions is inappropriate. But, whatever such theology might gain in divine invulnerability, it loses in pertinence to the human struggle with the problem of evil. Israel, itself, worked at explaining what this phenomenon was all about (Deuteronomy 7, 9), and we can do no less.

If these ways are not appropriate angles of vision on this phenomenon, what basic theological approaches might assist us? The most important are the following:

a) God has chosen to be dependent upon human beings in the achievement of goals in the world. Even where divine activity so fills the scene as it does in this text, the human element is not missing.

b) God works in the world with what is available, i.e., with human beings as they are, with all their foibles and flaws, and within societal structures, however inadequate. God wills righteous behavior from people, but must "make do" with whatever they come up with, including even using evil to achieve a redemptive purpose. God does not perfect these aspects of the world before working in and through them. This does not necessarily confer a positive value on those human means through which God chooses to work. Thus, the results of such work will always be mixed, and less than what would have happened had God chosen to act alone. Hence, as an example, there will be violence associated with God's work in the world because, to a greater or lesser degree, violence will be characteristic of those through whom the work is done.

Moreover, because societal structures are constantly changing, the "framing" within which God's work appears through the centuries will be quite diverse and complex. Thus, there is a contextual character to the work of God in the world. That is to say, if "holy war" (or the monarchy) is a societal structure in ancient Israel, then God's work (indeed, sovereignty) in the world is conditioned by, limited by, that structure in that time and place.

• If "holy war" is not an existing structure in a society, God will be at work through other given structures; but, given the variety of structures in the Bible, there is nothing sacred about a particular structure of Israelite society so that one should seek to transfer it to other societies. Thus, one should not attempt to create a holy war structure in a society where it is non-existent just so that God might be at work in more "biblical" ways, any more than one should create a monarchy.

c) Human beings will never have a perfect perception of how they are to serve as God's instruments in the world. Each perception will have been informed in significant ways by the context of which it was a part. It is very difficult to evaluate such perceptions because our context is not that of Israel's. Yet, it is helpful to remember that Israel's interpretation of what God was about in the world, and in the wars she fought, was conditioned by her context.

● In the biblical world such perceptions are commonly expressed as the direct speech of God. This often occasions a literalness in our understanding that can lead to unfortunate results. Today, we use the direct speech of God much less often (e.g., "I forgive you all your sins"), and when we do, we normally understand that we have not heard such a word directly, but that it is an insight gained through study and reflection upon the tradition. The direct speech of God in the Bible should be understood in comparable ways.

d) Israel gave a twofold theological rationale for waging the wars against the Canaanites in the way it did. First, so that Israel might not be led astray by the seductive religious practices of the Canaanites (Deut 7:1-5, 16). Second, as instruments of the judgment of God, exacted because of the wickedness of the Canaanites (Deut 9:4-5), and not because Israel deserved to possess the land. It is primarily in those terms (that is, judgment upon the quintessence of evil) that one must seek to understand the matter from Israel's perspective.

● Divine judgment in the OT was thought to be enacted within history, and not in some after-life. This made for a decisiveness of action that was not common in the NT literature. Nevertheless, apocalyptic writing and the NT have an even more severe understanding of judgment; consigning the wicked to the eternal fires of hell. Thus, whether in the promised land or in heaven, utopia might be thought possible only by means of radical surgery. Joshua could thus become a proof-text for the true revolutionaries among us.

It is important to realize that Israel did not understand such judgment in a narrow way, as if it were exempt from such a possibility in its own future. Deuteronomy 28 makes it very clear that Israel could become the object of the very same judgmental activity of God.

In a related matter, it might be noted that Israel did not believe that God was narrowly involved only with Israel in such displacing/possessing activity in relationship to a land (see Deut 2:5, 9, 12, 23); God's involvement in the military activities of the nations of the world is also characteristic of prophetic thought (see Amos 9:7; Isa 10, 45:1).

> ● Such seeming confidence in the interpretation of *how* God is involved in the activities of the nations is strange to many modern ears (though it is common among some of the modern apocalyptic interpretations). But, *that* God is pervasively involved in the life of all individuals and societies, working to achieve good purposes, can be confessed without difficulty.

e) Holy war must be assessed in terms that recognize that Israel was, for much of its history, a nation/state, and not a church or the Kingdom of God on earth. One simply has to recognize that with Israel's world being the way it was, war (along with other trappings of government) was necessary for Israel's survival. While Israel at times erred in confusing the nation/state with the "people of God," the prophets, in particular, castigated those who would confuse or identify them. How Israel as a state waged war against non-Canaanite nations is not so much the problem (cf. Deut 20:10-14); it was the way in which the post-Exodus community waged war against the Canaanites. Yet, however mistaken Israel may have been with respect to the severity of such wars, it was believed to be a matter of its survival as a people.

f) That God would stoop to become involved in such realities as war is finally not a matter for despair, but of hope. For God to be absent from such aspects of the life of the world would be to give the world up to its own violence. But, God being involved in the evil of the world means that evil is not the last word. What a greater tragedy war would be if God were not involved, struggling in that human violence to bring about good ends.

> ● Just as God's active presence in the death of Jesus is said to have brought life to the world, so also it might be said that divine involvement in war, in that miasma of suffering and death, makes for the possibility that life and good will eventually emerge, and not tragedy alone. In everything, including war, God seeks to accomplish a loving purpose in the world.

Moreover, because of the presence of evil in this world, for God to work toward redemptive goals inevitably involves conflict and violence; the forces of evil will not surrender voluntarily. Thus, such conflict is necessary in order to prevent an even greater evil.

g) By participating in history, by becoming involved in all that occurs, God takes the road of suffering and death. Through such involvement, God not only uses flawed human efforts, but also absorbs the effects of their sinfulness and thus suffers violence. God's vulnerability is strikingly evident in the fact that the gift of the land entailed the evil effects of war. God thus not only takes on the sufferings perpetrated as a result of such activity, but also assumes part of the culpability for it in the fact that a divine gift lies behind the whole affair.

Finally, we need to suggest what kind of word this text would have brought to the exiles in Babylon.

First and foremost, it would seem, it addressed the issue of powerlessness. Israel ought not despair regarding the divine promises because of its lowly situation. God is at work in the world to fulfill promises, and they will come to fulfillment even in the face of powerful opposition. Again, the basic response of the people is to trust in God and be obedient to leaders sent by God.

The liturgical character of the text might also have suggested to them that God works in salvific ways in, and through, the life of worship, making past redemptive actions real in the present. Faithful attentiveness to matters of worship is important, if God has chosen to use such a means for the fulfillment of promises to the people. In the activity of worship the power of God is at work in the community of faith, and it has effects beyond their imagining.

Moreover, this text (along with chap. 2) may have been intended to address tensions between the exiles and people in the land of Canaan. As the exiles think about a future in that land, they need to recognize that persons of faith have been there all along, and ought to be incorporated into any planned community. They may not conform to standards of purity that are now matters of concern to the exilic community, but they, too, may have been the recipients of divine promises, and may be of much help in the return to the land.

While the matter of holy war does not seem to have functioned in a paradigmatic way for the exiles in their return to the land (though see Jer 29:16-20), all the dangers inherent in any indiscriminate mixing with the idolatrous elements of the population are made evident throughout the deuteronomic history (note also that interest in rebuilding the temple upon their return would find support in Josh 6:19, 24).

Worshiping God Alone (Joshua 24:1-28)

The exiles, those who were now quite literally "beyond the River" Euphrates (vv 2, 3, 14, 15), would have found in the material of this chapter some striking responses to their concerns.

How was God to be worshiped in this strange land? The exiles were surrounded by the worship of the gods of their captors; was it legitimate, in a fashion typical in their world, to mix elements from the worship of these gods with the worship of Yahweh? What difference would it make?

How is it possible to justify such extreme judgmental actions as had been taken toward those whom the deity had called? Israel alone had Yahweh known of all the families of the earth (Amos 3:2), so why would they be punished for all their inquities? Given their status, they had no idea that their idolatries would lead to such harsh consequences. If their case were brought into a court of law, they could plead ignorance; who would witness against them besides the defendant, God himself?

Along with chap. 23, this material is represented as the last action of Joshua before his death, a last will and testament (cf. Genesis 48–49; Deuteronomy 32–33). While the parallels between 23:1-2 and 24:1 suggest that these chapters once functioned separately as alternative conclusions to this segment of the story, they are now presented as two different, but related, events.

● One way of understanding their present relationship is in terms of the exilic context to which the author addresses himself. Chapter 23 tends to be an explanation, thrice repeated, of why the people "perished from off this good land" (vv 13, 15, 16): because of their worship of other gods. Yet, the chapter is oriented toward the future, with the continued articulation of the promise and the importance of faithfulness. Chapter 24, then, constitutes a proper response of the community to these concerns, as they give their public commitment before God and each other regarding how their lives might be shaped to make that future possible.

Unlike chap. 23, which is entirely the composition of the deuteronomic historian, with its typical vocabulary and phrasing, chap. 24 has a more complicated history. While it appears that the historian has touched up the material (cf. vv 13, 20, 24), the vast bulk of it is reflective of much older traditions. The chapter may have been integral to the Elohistic source of the Pentateuch, and thus have functioned in the context of the struggle with Baal worshipers at the time of Elijah (see 1 Kgs 18:21).

The most common scholarly conclusion is that this chapter has its ultimate roots in a covenant-making ceremony in early Israel. As such, it may report a constitutive ceremony, which unified the various tribal units to form "all Israel" under the suzerainty of Yahweh, the God of the Joshua "household" (i.e., house of Joseph). Alternatively, it may be a covenant renewal ceremony, which was held with some regularity at a central sanctuary of the tribal league (see 8:30-35, which bears an uncertain relationship to this chapter), the most basic purpose of which was to renew the people's relationship with God.

There are some problems with these two approaches, however. Against the first option, there is nothing in the text to suggest that this is a constitutive assembly, bringing diverse tribal units together. All of the peoples gathered at the assembly are Yahweh worshipers; as vv 16, 20 make clear, the issue is one of "forsaking" Yahweh. Over against the second option, there is no sign in the text that this reports the renewal of a previously concluded covenant. While a formal religious service is spoken of (v 1, "they presented themselves before God"), a more focused concern seems to be in view.

In addition, the covenant-making structure so often spoken of in connection with this chapter is not so clearly present as is commonly thought. The general form such a covenant would have taken, as shown by ancient Near Eastern parallels, is: preamble, historical prologue (reciting superior's beneficial actions), stipulations (obligations placed on subjects) followed by an oath, provision for preservation of covenant document and for its public reading, a list of witnesses, and curses and blessings for violation or fulfillment. While one can clearly discern a number of these elements in Joshua 24, the chapter is more complex than the typical treaty form. Key elements are missing, or obscure, or out of order: the oath, the blessings and the curses, the stone as witness with the people themselves as witnesses, and the stipulations. Moreover, the fourfold exchange between

Joshua and people (vv 14-24) complicates the character of the event reported.

It seems best to conclude that the author of this chapter has picked up key elements from the treaty tradition, and used them to report an important, but singular, occasion of covenant-making, in the light of special circumstances faced by the early community.

The focus of this chapter is best seen in the light of the immediately preceding and following chapters (Joshua 22–23; Judges 2–3), namely, the proper worship of Yahweh. Joshua 22 speaks of a specific concern within the community regarding such worship (see vv 5, 16, 19, 22-29), with an important emphasis on witness (vv 27, 28, 34). Joshua 23 raises the most important issue for the future—serving other gods instead of, or along with, Yahweh (vv 7, 16). Judges 2–3 returns to this matter (2:7, 11, 13, 19, 3:6-7), and it then becomes a recurrent theme throughout the rest of the deuteronomic history (cf. pp. 21 ff.).

> ● Discussion of the larger literary context is important for interpretation. In the history of the story of Joshua 24, scholars have tended to deal with it in isolation from that context.

Joshua 24, with its fifteen (!) instances of the word "serve, worship," makes one clear point: the future of the community in the land is finally determined by whether it worships Yahweh alone, or turns to the worship of other gods (too). No stipulations or laws in the usual sense are presented, because it is a matter of *one* "statute and ordinance" (v 25, it is singular in the Hebrew), and that has to do with the proper worship of Yahweh. Joshua 24 thus stands where it most naturally should stand, at the juncture between the end of the conquest and the beginning of life in the land.

> ● The repetition of key vocabulary words is commonly a clue to the author's central concern.

A few words on the structure of this passage will be helpful. After the formal summoning of "all the people" to Shechem (v 1), God's good deeds on behalf of Israel are recited (vv 2-13). Verses 12-13 serve as a summary statement of what has most recently brought them to the present moment. Verses 14-24 consist of a dialogue with four exchanges (14-18; 19-21; 22, 22-24), with the persistent use of "serve, worship" serving as the focus in each. Verses 14 and 23-24 surround (in an ABBA pattern) this section, and demonstrate this focus. Verse 14: Serve the Lord, and put away other gods; vv 23-25: put away other gods, we will serve the Lord. Verses 25-28 provide a narrative conclusion.

We can now turn to a more detailed discussion of the ways in which the narrator develops his central concerns.

First of all, there is the recital in vv 2-13 (cf. Deut 26:5-10).

1) The depiction of God as speaker not only makes more forceful the import of what is said, but emphasizes that God is the one responsible for all these good developments in Israel's life. Moreover, it serves to stress that no other gods were involved in enabling this history, and hence it is to the Lord alone that Israel is to make her worshipful response. But even more, as the Word of God, it focuses attention on the proper human response. However much human leadership has played a role, when it comes to the act of worship, it is God alone who is to be praised. The fact that unlike Deuteronomy 26 and other recitals, this is the Word of God and not the people's confession, makes this an especially forthright proclamation of the gospel.

2) Emphasis upon God's good deeds focuses the chapter more clearly on the heart of the matter, namely, loyalty to God. Israel's realization of her faithlessness during all these gracious activities makes God's unmerited goodness stand out even more. Israel lives only because of the grace of God.

• The fact that the Sinai covenant event is not mentioned in historical recitals, here and elsewhere, has prompted efforts to separate the Sinai and conquest traditions from one another historically. Perhaps they are not sequential events in the life of a single group? This particular context may explain the omission, however, making the drawing of such historical conclusions inappropriate. The way in which a given passage functions in its own context must be determined as far as possible *before* tradition-historical conclusions such as the above are drawn from it.

3) The focus is on the fathers up through v 7*a* ("they"), but on those now present ("you") in vv 7*b*-13. Yet, in vv 5*b*-7, there is a mixing of the fathers and the present generation (vv 6*a*, 7*a*). Moreover, the present generation is seen as having been involved in the Exodus, though they were not literally there. This brings the nature of Israel's worship to the fore. Commonly, in Israel's worship (see Josh 4:22-23; Deut 5:2-3, 6:20-24; Ps 66:5-6, 114), past events are actualized. That is, they are made so real in the present context of worship that the worshipers understand themselves to be involved in those events, and thereby to be participating in the effects of the divine activity at work there. Such events are thus understood to be constitutive and salvific, not only for past generations, but for every generation of the people of God. In context, this gives the people historical depth so that they may see that it has always been Yahweh, and no other god, who has enabled their history.

At this point, it might be noted how important the use of the second person ("you") is throughout the chapter (and thus parallel to the way in which the material in Deuteronomy is put). The emphasis throughout is on motivating the people, encouraging response, moving the heart (see v 23), clarifying expectations; the narrative thus has a certain sermonic character (its nonauthoritarian approach is seen especially in v 15!). Moreover, the attention of the "you" is focused on relationship to Another, namely, God, and not on a relationship to a contract or agreement or to certain stipulations. Focus is thus upon personal loyalty.

4) The reference to the "other gods" which the fathers of Israel served is made explicit in the OT only here (Josh 24:2). It is picked up again in vv 14-15, where the more recent past in Egypt is incorporated. It then becomes a centerpiece for attention in what follows (vv 16, 20, 23, cf. v 27). The reason for picking up on that matter so forcefully relates again to the larger context,

namely, the concern about worshiping Yahweh or these other gods. We shall see later how this matter is an especially important concern for the audience in exile.

● The inclusion of this and other unique elements reveals the freedom that Israel believed it had in retelling old stories in order to make them speak to new situations in the life of the people of God. Such lack of rigidity, when combined with an absolute insistence on the exclusive worship of Yahweh, is an important model for every generation concerning priorities and freedom relative to the tradition.

Next is the dialogue between Joshua and the people (vv 14-24). Joshua exhorts the people to revere and to worship the Lord faithfully, which entails the putting away of other gods (v 14). The point is not that the cult of Yahweh was neglected (see vv 16, 20), but that it had become mixed up with the worship of other gods. It is in essence a call for adherence to the first commandment (a recurrent theme in the deuteronomic history, e.g., 1 Kgs 18:21; 2 Kings 17). It is not surprising that Israel would have a problem in this regard, for such exclusivism was unique in the ancient Near East. But, the insistence here is that no such syncretism is allowable in the worship of Yahweh. In fact, it is suggested that if they are going to incorporate elements of the worship of other gods, they should go the whole way and get rid of all Yahweh elements in their worship (v 15). This verse emphasizes that no coercion is involved; Joshua seeks to move the people to decide for themselves concerning this matter. The motivation for such exclusivism is the recital of God's gracious acts ("therefore," v 14). The gospel, not some arbitrary set of regulations or threats, is the basis for the call to hear and to worship Yahweh alone. Any human achievement or merit in this matter has been eliminated (vv 12-13).

It is a striking feature of the people's response (vv 16-18) that they grasp this latter point precisely. By repeating in their own words some of the key elements of God's activity on their behalf, they recognize these activities as constitutive of their faith and

life, making them the community that they are. They have been
made God's people ("for he is our God"), and "therefore" (v
18*b*) they will worship the Lord. The word of the gospel has
motivated this response.

> • The priority of God's grace is as central to the OT as it is to the
> NT. "Legalism" is a word which does not fit in any description of
> the faith and life of Israel.

One would have thought that this would be sufficient, but
another dialogue follows in vv 19-20. These very difficult verses
can best be understood if the key question is: *how* is God to be
worshiped? It is an emphasis made necessary in the light of
Israel's proclivities to idolatry.

Part of the problem in these verses may be translation. The
first line of Joshua's statement can be translated: "You cannot
serve the Lord" (RSV and most). Yet, it would be quite
anomalous for Joshua to ask the people to worship the Lord
(v 14), and acknowledge that choice (v 22), only to turn around
and say that this is impossible. Thus, this translation is possible,
and even likely, but only if it is understood as, "You cannot serve
the Lord as you seek to do at present, i.e., if you continue to mix
the worship of him with other gods." Otherwise, one could go in
the direction of the TEV translation, "You may not be able to
serve the Lord," thus expressing Joshua's doubts in their ability
or willingness to worship the Lord alone, given their past history.

> • In difficult passages such as this, it is often helpful to consult
> various translations.

The point is not that the worship of a holy and jealous God is
impossible, but that it is a very serious matter, needing special
attentiveness. God is a holy God, whose uniqueness would be
compromised by idolatrous forms of worship. God is a jealous
God, and such forms of worship would compromise the people's
loyalty. In either case, the kind of God in whom they believe
makes an idolatrous situation intolerable.

Given the already evident propensities of the people to take a syncretistic direction in their worship, it may be that they will not be able to worship Yahweh as it must be done, and hence the only possible direction for the people to take is the option provided for in v 15. It is an either/or situation for the people; they are faced with a choice which must be made. They cannot "go limping with two different opinions. If the Lord is God, follow him; but if Baal, then follow him" (1 Kgs 18:21); no middle ground is possible.

"He will not forgive (or bear) your transgressions or sins." This is also difficult to understand. The meaning might well be: he will not bear your sins continuously—see Isa 1:14; Jer 44:22; Num 14:13-25. One needs to reckon with an end to the divine patience. In effect, the people ought not try to live close to the margin of God's patience. Their sins will not be carried forever.

● This close connection between serving other gods, God as jealous, and God as one who will eventually visit the iniquity of the fathers upon the children is also found in Deut 5:9-10 (cf. Exod 34:6-8). Israel is free to reject Yahweh and go after other gods, but she needs to recognize that this will lead to disaster. God, after much patience, will finally honor that rejection and let his people reap the consequences of their sins.

This should not be interpreted as Joshua laying a dire threat upon the people, however. In context, it is a way of stressing the seriousness of the choice the people are making. It is comparable to the point made in Amos 3:2. To make the commitment to Yahweh is a serious matter, because the effects of brokenness will be all the more severe if, and when, rejection of Yahweh occurs. Those who make the choice for Yahweh and then depart from it are worse off than if they had left it alone. (An analogy may be made with divorce, which has effects more dire than those which follow upon the breaking of a relationship which is not so close and intimate.)

In the face of this note of seriousness, the people are insistent; they reiterate their commitment to worship Yahweh alone.

In the light of this understanding, v 22 makes clear sense. The people have been made aware of all the implications of this commitment. Upon this, Joshua indicates to them that their own words will serve as a witness to their understanding that there can be no compromise in the worship of Yahweh. Thus, should the day of judgment come, they would not be able to say: We were not aware of how serious this relationship with God was. Nor could they accuse God of injustice upon suffering such a judgment, as if God were guilty and they innocent, because they didn't know what they were getting into. Once again, the people agree that they have understood all that is at stake in this matter.

Verses 23-24 then return to the beginning of the dialogue, with a request to act in some formal way with respect to their involvement with other gods. If the parallel in Gen 35:2-4 can be called upon, the response of the people in v 24 was accompanied by a symbolic act of burying all objects connected with such worship (note that the oak of Gen 35:6 is mentioned in v 26). That all of this is directed to the hearts of those involved is made clear in v 23*b* (cf. 1 Kgs 8:58; 11:2-4); this is not to be some external response, as if to some formal agreement. Unless their hearts are in it, it is of no avail.

● One cannot help but be struck by the similarity of this dialogue with John 21:15-17, and Jesus' threefold questioning of Peter regarding his love.

The final section, vv 25-28, concludes the narrative. Joshua is seen as the one who mediated the covenant for the people. There is now one "statute and ordinance" to which they have committed themselves: the worship of Yahweh alone. They have chosen to have no other gods.

Joshua now moves to make a permanent record of this commitment. He writes it in a covenant document ("book"); it would appear that a record of this commitment is now preserved along with other Torah materials to which the people have committed themselves (see Deut 31:24-26, and the concern for a "witness" in the light of the inclinations of the people to rebellion). As if to multiply the witnesses, a stone is erected as a memorial. It is striking to note that the stone is represented as being able to hear and witness: elements of the natural order are here drawn into the God-human relationship, thus testifying to the cosmic effects which this commitment has.

Finally, we need to turn again to the audience for which this narrative was finally prepared: the exiles.

Generally, it may be noted how striking the parallels are between the early Israelite community and the exiles. They, too, were faced with the question of the proper worship of Yahweh in the midst of a culture which worshiped other gods. Indeed, some syncretistic practices had begun to emerge in the worship life of the exilic community (see Jer 44:15-19; Isa 40:18-20; 44:9-20). The issue of the proper worship was an especially urgent one, and that may explain the mention of other gods served "beyond the River" (where the exiles now were!). The word which this narrative brings to such a situation is that there can be no mixing of the worship of Yahweh with that of other gods. The exiles have the choice of clinging to the worship of Yahweh alone, of putting away whatever syncretistic elements may have crept into their worship life, or moving wholeheartedly to the worship of foreign gods.

This chapter thus constitutes a paradigm for the kind of commitment called for on the part of the exiles: Worship Yahweh, and Yahweh alone.

It is striking that the confession of the people in vv 16-18 is so applicable to the exilic situation: the people confess that God has "preserved us in all the way that we went, and among all the peoples through whom we passed." If the exiles were to think clearly about all that God had done for them (and the use of "you" in the recital of vv 2-13 would have been heard as including them), even in such trials that recent events had occasioned for them, they could make a comparable confession. Moreover, the fact that God had been so active on behalf of the people outside the promised land would have been heard in relation to their present place away from home. God works for the chosen wherever they are.

This confession is not unimportant for the future which the

exiles faced. They would certainly have realized that it was just such a turning away from Yahweh that had made for the recent tragedy. And so, they would have known that the words of vv 19-20 were especially applicable for their future as well. Commitment to the worship of Yahweh alone would make a difference with respect to the shape of that future.

This chapter also addresses another issue that had surfaced among the exiles, viz., the question of the justice of God (Ezek 18:2, 25; Lam 5:7). Joshua 24:22, and the great concern for specifying witnesses, may well have served to meet this issue. The people knew full well the implications of their past commitment to Yahweh; they could not plead ignorance or accuse God of injustice. This would help explain not only the past, but make the shape of their future clear as well.

● The various elements noted in the message of the text for the exiles constitute points at which the text might also be appropriated today. It is an instance of the importance of the first commandment for those who worship God. It is not enough to worship God, in view of this commandment. Neither faith in God, nor the strength of that faith, guarantees right action. It is a question finally of the *kind* of God you believe in. While the OT may often speak of idols in this connection, in a more sophisticated, modern society it is often a question of "making up" one's own gods, that is, conceiving of God in terms of images that have little or nothing to do with the kind of God revealed in the Bible. Thus, this text would insist on the worship of a certain kind of God. The basic image being that of a God who has been with, and for, the people throughout all of their journeys, and bestowed on them the gift of salvation quite apart from their deserving. The gospel must thus be at the center of their imagery and their worship of God.

THE BOOK OF JUDGES

God's Unpredictability (Judges 2:6–3:6)

How tempting it is to misuse a passage like this one! It would appear from a cursory reading of the text that a life with God can be mechanically conceived. Be obedient and God will act positively toward you, letting you live in peace; be disobedient and God will bring the roof down upon your heads. It would almost appear to fit into our computerized age; everything, including the relationship with God, can finally be reduced to a fine science, where every piece of a puzzle is made to fit. On the surface of things, that would appear to be a very comforting way to proceed. You never have to wonder about God's way with the world; it is a cut-and-dried affair. All one has to do is conform to the system, and all will be well. And, on the other side, you can be assured that for those who don't conform, they will receive their just desserts. But, is this the case?

First of all, we need to take a look at the larger context of which this text is a part. One of the first things that strikes one in such a comparison is that chap. 1 and chaps. 3ff. are filled with the activities of specific persons or tribes, while this text is generalized. It speaks of enemies, plunderers, nations, judges, sins, and the people of Israel. Generic references abound. Moreover, there is a lack of temporal reference, except in the most general of terms. Thus, the text would appear to give us a panoramic vision of what is characteristic of a variety of situations in Israel, perhaps not only during this time, but in any time of the people of God.

1. Relationship with preceding materials. This is a very difficult matter to sort out, finally, not least because with 2:6 we are brought back to a time before 1:1 (which speaks of the death of Joshua). Verses 6-9 (which may originally have followed Joshua 23) essentially reiterate Josh 24:28-31 (in the order 28, 31, 29, 30). One key to seeing the ordering of these materials is to note the three stages in vv 6, 10: (a) the days of Joshua; (b) the days of the elders who outlived Joshua; (c) "another generation after them who did not know the Lord."

Joshua 23 makes it clear that there were indigenous peoples still remaining in the land of Canaan at the time of Joshua's death (vv 4, 12). Judges 1 would thus be seen as the picking up of that population-problem under "the elders who outlived Joshua" (e.g., Caleb in 1:11ff.).

● Scholars commonly conclude that this chapter is actually an older, more realistic version of the settlement than the one recorded in Joshua. That may well be, and it will affect one's reconstruction of Israel's early history in the land. Our concern here, however, is the function of these materials in their present literary context (cf. pp. 52-53).

The few explicitly theological references in chap. 1 (vv 2, 4, 19, 22) indicate that even though the Lord was with them, they did not drive out all the inhabitants. It was not, however, that the Israelites *could not* drive them out, but that they *did not*. Given the Lord's presence and promise (cf. Josh 23:5), the latter seems certain. This is also suggested by the references to forced labor in vv 28, 30, 33, 35. If they were able to put them to forced labor, they certainly could have driven them out, and failure to do so was contrary to God's command that they not be "mixed with," or "join the remnant of," or "take wives from" the remaining peoples of the land (cf. Josh 23:7, 12).

This approach to chap. 1 then helps us understand 2:1-5, a unit which picks up from chap. 1 and explains what is to follow. Verse 2 suggests that the actions of chap. 1 have entailed making a covenant with the people of the land; their continued presence means also the presence of their altars (though no idolatrous activity is alluded to). Because of this disobedient action, the realities intimated in Josh 23:13 are now upon them: "they shall be a snare and a trap for you, a scourge on your sides, and thorns in your eyes." 2:1-5 thus makes it clear why the Canaanites and their gods will become a constant source of temptation to them, and to which they will succumb again and again. At the same time, v 1c strikes a different note: "I will never break my covenant with you." Thus, in the chapters which follow, we will be witness to a profound mercy in the face of continued apostasy. Thus, finally, 1:1–2:5 functions, not as a paradigm for the chapters which follow, but as an explanation of a situation which prevails in "the days of the elders who outlived Joshua," and which occasions all the difficulties that are now to follow. The die was cast; not even the people's repentance could reverse things.

Now the function of 2:6-10 becomes clearer. In almost flashback fashion, vv 6-9 serve to recapitulate the most recent stage in Israel's history, and then with v 10 a new subject is introduced: the new generation which had not directly experienced the work of God in the conquest. Verse 11 then characterizes the period to come in language typical of the various stories of the judges (see 3:7, 11; 4:1).

2. Relationship with following materials. These verses appear to give the basic framework for the stories of many of the judges (the final reference is in 13:1, and there much abbreviated). See Deut 4:25-31 for the pattern, as well.

a. The people of Israel "did what was evil in the sight of the Lord," serving other gods (2:11, 3:7, 4:1, etc.).

b. God is provoked to anger, and he delivers them into the hands of their enemies (2:14; 3:8; 10:7).

c. The people cry out because of their affliction; God is moved to pity them, sends a judge to deliver them from their troubles, and the land has rest (2:18b; 3:9; 6:7ff.).

d. When the judge dies, the people lapse into even greater idolatry (2:19), and the cycle begins all over again.

At the same time, it must be noted that the framework is not as schematized as is commonly suggested. One of the more interesting variations is in the third component of the framework, the crying of the people to God. This element is barely present in this text. There is a possible allusion in 2:15, "they were in sore straits." But, it is important to note that the Lord raises up judges without any reference to the response of the people. The only other reference is the phrase, "by their groaning," in v 18 (a word not used elsewhere in the book). It is sometimes suggested that this third element in the framework contains the note of penitence. But the only story in Judges that has reference to penitence is that of Jephthah (10:10-15). And, even in the latter text, the matter which *finally* moves the Lord to act is not the repentance of the people, but their "misery" (10:16). Moreover, the story of Jephthah makes it clear that God's response to the cries of his people is not an automatic thing, even if they repent with all sincerity.

The very minor role of the response of the people in this chapter, with the complete absence of the repentance motif, provides an interpretative key for the rest of the book: it is the gracious and merciful action of God which alone carries Israel through from one generation to the next. God acts on behalf of the people quite apart from whether they have repented, or turned from their wicked ways.

It is, also, to be noted that never in this text (and elsewhere only in 10:16) is it said that the people turned from their idolatrous ways and served the Lord. Thus, 2:19b, "they did not drop any of their practices or their stubborn ways," should be seen as basically descriptive of the entire period. The evil perpetrated by the people is rather more constant than an up-and-down cycle of rebellion, repentance, rebellion. Verse 19a (as also 10:13) suggests rather an ever-increasing rebellion, an intensification of continuing practice (the relationship between 6:7 and 6:30, as well as between 8:27 and 8:33ff. reinforces this understanding). Throughout this period, the people of Israel "did not listen to their judges" (2:17a); they didn't even wait until after the judge had died. "Every man did what was right in his own eyes" (17:6, 21:25).

With this rather extended look at the context behind us, let us now concentrate initially upon 2:11-20a. It is a highly repetitive section. This might best be explained in terms of a redactor weaving various traditions together in such a way as to impress his audience with the force of the issue: the effects of disloyalty to Yahweh are grave indeed. An attempt to outline the passage may reveal some logic in that weaving.

1. People do evil in the sight of the Lord (vv 11-13).
    a. *Served* the Baals (v 11b).
        b. *Forsook* the Lord who delivered them (v 12a).
            c. Served other gods—provoking the Lord to anger (v 12bc).
        b. *Forsook the Lord* (v 13a).
    a. *Served* the Baals and the Ashtaroth (v 13b).
2. The aftermath of the people's disloyalty (vv 14-20a).
    a. *The anger of the Lord is kindled* (v. 14a—anticipated in v 12c).
        b. He gave them into *the hand of plunderers.*
        He sold them into *the hand of their enemies* (v 14bc).
        (Whenever . . . *the Lord was against* them—v 15a).
            c. They were in sore straits (v 15b).
        b. The Lord raised up judges (v 16a).
        . . . To save them from *the hand of the plunderers* (v 16b).
        . . . they *served other gods,* turning aside from the way of *their fathers* (v 17).
        (Whenever . . . *the Lord was with* the judge—v 18a).
        . . . He saved them from *the hand of their enemies* (v 18b).
        . . . they turned back from *their fathers, serving other gods* (v 19).
    a. *The anger of the Lord is kindled* (v 20a).
3. Divine decision (vv 20b-23).
    a. People transgressed the covenant of *the fathers* (v 20b).
        b. I will *not drive out nations Joshua* left (v 21).
            c. That by them I may test Israel (v 22a).

   b. Whether to walk in the way as *their fathers* (v 22*b*).
  a. Lord will *not drive out nations* now as with *Joshua* (v 23).

A few observations about this structure. Verses 11-13 might seem overly repetitive, but the *abcba* structure serves as a literary device to intensify the disloyalty of the people. This statement immediately follows upon a reference to all that the Lord had accomplished on behalf of Israel. A comparable juxtaposition of the gracious work of God and the disloyalty of the people is repeated in vv 16/17 and 18/19. This repetitiveness would serve to underscore the utter ungratefulness of the people. And the whole series is topped off with the comment: They did not drop any of their practices or their stubborn ways (v 19*b*).

The divine anger emerges in the outline at two points, issuing in two different divine responses. In the first instance (v 14*a*), the divine anger issues in a judgment that takes the form of defeat at the hand of their enemies, resulting finally in the "sore straits" of the people. The salvific actions of God follow. The repeated saving actions of vv 16 and 18 are certainly intended to demonstrate the graciousness of God in the face of continued apostasy. That is, one would have expected another indication of divine judgment after v 17. But such is not the case. God responds, not with anger and judgment, but with a continued raising up of judges. The stress thus falls on the *lack* of any rhythm of human sinfulness and divine judgment (continued oppression is noted in v 18*b*, but it is not specified as divine judgment). What comes through is the divine patience: God continues to save them from the hands of their enemies in spite of continued apostasy. The return to the theme of divine anger in v 20 signals a new stage in the divine response. A new turn is taken: God determines that the future will now take a certain shape. The verses that follow are largely repetitive of 2:2-3 in terms of basic content, but there are two new elements. (1) The place of the other nations in the land is now made a permanent matter, "I will not *henceforth* . . ." Israel is stuck with this situation. (2) The presence of these nations is seen to have the function of testing the fidelity of Israel to her God.

The reason for the divine anger is rooted in the people's turning to other gods (a theme recurring throughout the deuteronomic history, e.g., 2 Kgs 13:3; 17:15ff.; 23:26). Fundamentally, this anger has reference to the fact that evil must not be allowed to have its own way with the world. Divine anger is thus a witness to God's refusal to acquiesce in the face of the power of evil in the life of the people; it is thus finally rooted in a concern for life rather than death. It becomes apparent quickly in this text that God's purposes are not annihilation, but that on the far side of the experience of judgment there might be restoration of the relationship which God intended.

God uses a variety of means to achieve such purposes. Here other nations become instruments of the divine discipline. On the whole, however, God's own activity is described in rather passive terms. God "gives them over" to the hands of their enemies so that they can no longer resist them. In essence this means that God "backs off" from providing a protective role, and lets Israel's enemies have their way. Or, God "leaves" the nations in the land, "not driving them out." The images of divine judgment are thus all passive. God does not "take the offensive" in judgment; there is no more standing in the breach, defending against the forces of evil and chaos in Israel's life. At the same time, while the divine action is passive, it is also personal. There is a decision to withdraw from the proximity of a personal relationship.

● It is always striking to moderns how assured Israel's theologians were in their understanding of the significance of historical movements. Israel's experience of oppression at the hands of her enemies is confidently interpreted in terms of judgment for Israel's apostasy. It occasions wonder because drawing such conclusions in contemporary situations is so difficult for us. But it has its roots in a fundamental confidence regarding God's thoroughgoing involvement in all aspects of life, not least in "seeing to" the maintenance of a moral order of things. They saw a continuum in the relationship between sin and the evil effects of sin, the latter often being understood in terms of judgment. While we may not be able to

speak today with the same confidence regarding God's involvement, or so closely connect community disaster with community
sin, there is a fundamental truth to be seen in the fact that God is
unrestingly working to rid the world of evil.

At the same time, it is clear from these texts that the judgment
of God is not capricious. As v 15 in particular makes clear: God
had warned them. Thus, the experience of judgment was no
surprise to the community. Again, the graciousness of God lies at
the root of things: only love is concerned enough to warn.

And then we are provided with what would appear to be a
contradictory picture. The God who judges hears the cries of his
people experiencing the distress of judgment, and seeks to
deliver them from it. It is almost as if God now moves in to
deliver the people from the effects of divine judgment. And so it
is. This makes it very clear that the divine judgment is not
considered to be an end in itself, as if God had no concerns
beyond judgment. Judgment there must be; evil must not be
allowed to go unchecked in the world. But judgment is not the
end of things for God. Once that judgment has been
experienced, and indeed in the midst of the very experience of
judgment, God is working graciously for deliverance. Deliverance is what God truly desires for the people. But, finally, it is
only in and through the experience of oppression and death, that
the experience of deliverance is possible. There can be no direct
move from apostasy to deliverance, except through judgment.
And so the judging activity of God is finally motivated by
gracious purposes. And the degree to which one discerns
repetition in these texts with regard to the sin-judgment-
deliverance cycle is finally a witness to the incredible mercy of
God in desiring life, and not death, for the people.

The language used to describe the movement of God in this
process is especially striking: God is "moved to pity" (v 18). The
judgment of God is always accompanied by the grief of God.
God's response is anything but mechanically conceived. Far from
any schema to which God is tied in relating to the people, here
the response is out of the depths of the divine heart. Hence,

God's gracious response is not something which is dictated by necessity. God neither *has* to respond in this manner, nor has anything that the people have done been sufficient to occasion such a response. Neither human obedience, nor human repentance, provides the final or sufficient motivation for the divine action. It is, finally, because God is moved by the desperate straits of the people, and the foundation for such merciful action is God's love and desire for their life.

● It is this "moved to pity" motif that is an important point for any appropriation of this text today. God's responses in relationship to the community are not determined according to some retributionary schematic. This is a highly personal relationship, far removed from any mechanical notions. God is revealed as one who is caught up by the situation, who is genuinely anguished over what has occurred, and is moved out of love to take action. This motif is repeated in 10:16 (cf. the JB's translation, "he could bear their sufferings no longer").

In the context of exile, it is at this latter point where the special word lies. The word is finally a word of hope. In the midst of repeated rejection on the part of the people, a disloyalty which has led to the severest forms of oppression in exile, there is here a word that makes it clear that judgment is not God's last word. God is a God of compassion, and that such compassion has become operative in their lives in the past, in the face of repeated apostasy, is a hope to cling to in times of despair. God will once again raise up a deliverer, not finally because of anything which they have done or will do, but because God is moved to do so out of love.

The roots of the divine judgment are to be found in the people's sin. The shape that this sin has taken is described in various ways in this chapter, but (as we have seen in Joshua 24) it boils down to one word: disloyalty. In vv 11ff., it is seen in terms of forsaking the God who had delivered them and going after other gods. Thus, the problem is seen to be not disobedience of some set of external regulations, but a rebellion against the graciousness of God, this God who has done so much for them (see Joshua 24 in particular). In the language of Joshua 23, the people have not "cleaved to the Lord your God" (v 8), and have not "loved the Lord your God" (v 11). The transgression of the covenant is defined in very narrow terms, "to go and serve other gods and bow down to them" (23:16). This "harlotry" (2:17) has issued in the disobedience of commandments, but the latter are only symptomatic of the much more fundamental problem: unfaithfulness. Thus, the only proper response of the people is first and foremost, not obedience, but a turning to God in repentance (cf. 10:10-16).

It may seem contradictory for God to decide to leave the people who are the source of idolatry in the land, when that very source has led to the people's defection. But these texts are informed by the realities of the situation: the peoples had not in fact been swept clean from the land. Their presence is in fact due to Israel's unfaithfulness, and this unfaithfulness may become endemic by their continued presence. But the latter is not necessarily the case; the people *could* remain loyal in the face of such temptation. The Canaanites' presence in the land is, thus, seen to provide a testing point for Israel (2:22; 3:1, 4). This was not understood to be something which God wanted for the people; what was desired throughout was to rid the land of any sort of temptation. Nevertheless, God makes use of the results of a situation, which are not commensurate with the original intention. Their presence in the land becomes a touchstone for sharpening Israel's own faithfulness. The fact that this development has its roots in the divine anger (v 20*a*) indicates that the testing was far from God's intention for Israel, but it becomes a means now used for salutary purposes. As Deut 8:16 (cf. 8:2; 13:4) makes clear, God's use of such testing is "to do you good in the end." Thus, God seeks to bring good out of evil, as always.

● It would be a tragic use of this text to suggest that God's testing is somehow to provide a stumbling block for people, to see if they can be lured into something (like some ancient "sting" operation). God is working with the realities of the situation, a temptation-filled situation which has been occasioned by the disloyalty of the people. The *use* of such a situation is for positive purposes: to sharpen their sensitivities in relationship to God. God's testing is thus finally concerned to bring good out of a situation that would otherwise only be filled with judgment.

The statements in 3:1-2 about the learning of war need to be placed within the context of such testing. Again, it is a matter of God working with the world as it is, of using existing conditions for good purposes. It will certainly be the case that Israel will henceforth be living in a hostile environment, beset before and behind by peoples who threaten their very existence. In order for Israel to be able to stand up to such forces of hostility, it is necessary that she learn about these aspects of warfare that will make such resistance, at least, possible. Thus, God again makes use of a situation fraught with negative possibilities to achieve some good, namely, the enabling of Israel to survive amid all the evil that threatens her continued life.

● Living in an age where war, particularly of the nuclear variety, threatens to undo the entire created order, it is difficult for us to read this text without flinching. What kind of a God is it who would teach people war! It is very important not to generalize from the concern in this text to a statement about what God is about in every age. The text is concerned with Israel's survival in that era, given that particular set of circumstances. The text is thus permeated by a sober realism with regard to that particular time and place. But its roots must not be forgotten; such a concern about war is necessary only because of Israel's disobedience. In order to achieve certain purposes, however, God in effect "gets his hands dirty." It is necessary to enter into this very compromised situation into which Israel has gotten herself, and work within it to bring about the survival necessary for Israel someday to be what she was called to be.

It should be clear from this study that there is no simple rhythmic understanding of the God-Israel relationship that is set forth in this text. We have seen how God's involvement in

Israel's life is not patterned according to any schema. God responds in salvific ways quite apart from the community's positive response; God's mercy and patience prevail in the face of continual apostasy; God allows for and indeed enables ongoing life, though only death is deserved. The import, finally, of such "unpredictable" responses is a witness to the incredible mercy of God, which goes beyond justice again and again. If God had chosen to abide by some immutable law of retribution, Israel would not have lasted a generation. Any analogy with human justice goes by the boards in the light of the terrible speed of the mercy of God.

It is thus apparent that one cannot make sense of the history of Israel simply in terms of her obedience and disobedience to God. In spite of much disobedience, Israel continued to survive. Whatever successes Israel had could in no significant way be ascribed to her own obedient action. Israel's failures often issue in one kind of disaster or another, but there is no predictable pattern. There is nothing in Israel's behavior that *finally* explains her existence. Israel's continued life is a mystery hidden deep within the gracious purposes of God: "I will never break my covenant with you" (2:1). To exiles in particular, this was an important word to hear.

● These last few paragraphs provide a number of points at which a rather immediate appropriation of this text is possible for today. God's people, again and again, exhibit patterns of life which threaten their existence. God's response is remarkable in its variety and flexibility, in order to accomplish salutary purposes. A highly personal divine response is revealed, which values mercy above retribution; we see a God who chooses to experience suffering rather than visit the people with the finality of death; we are surprised by a God who finds ways of working in, with, and under very compromising situations in which people have placed themselves in order to bring about good. In the midst of unfaithfulness, the faithfulness of God is revealed, a God who never breaks covenant. Only in such a God is hope to be found.

THE BOOKS OF SAMUEL

God Provides New Leadership (1 Samuel 3:1-10)

Certainly every Sunday school series in the land must use this text as an example-story. It is easy to visualize some artist's version of a boy about twelve years of age, serving in the temple in some capacity—a model of piety for all twelve-year-olds today. Is that a proper use of this story?

> • This picture of Samuel has probably been influenced strongly by the fact that the Gospel of Luke uses language from this story to portray Jesus' appearance in the temple as a twelve-year-old (see Luke 2:40-52, esp. comparing v 52 with 1 Sam 2:26).

Once again we ask what questions were being raised by the exilic audience to which this material might have responded. It is clear that the leadership, particularly the religious leadership, in the years before the Exile, led the people in ways that were often corrupt and idolatrous (see 2:12). What structure would best guard against that happening again? An even more basic question might well have emerged for the exiles: Given this corruption and consequent judgment, can God be counted on to raise up new leaders for the community of faith? This time of judgment has certainly meant that "the word of the Lord is rare . . . there is no frequent vision" (3:1). Will God once again speak to the people? If so, how might this be accomplished?

While the focus is on leadership, the theme of bringing down the wicked and raising up the lowly (2:1-10) would have responded to more general questions raised by the exiles. How is God at work in the present situation? How do such lowly ones fit into the divine plans?

It is very important to place this text within the larger context of chaps. 1:1–4:1a. It is commonly thought by scholars that the bulk of this section constitutes the basic textual unit, generally given a quite early date, with 2:1-10, portions of 2:27-36 and 3:11-14, 19ff., having been added along the way (probably by the deuteronomic historian).

● It seems likely that the first of these added passages is used by the final redactor for theological purposes (see below). The second passage appears to have been expanded from an original oracle that focused on Eli, with the promise pertaining to Samuel (cf. 2:35a), to one which seemingly anticipates later developments in the priesthood: the deposing of Abiathar (1 Kgs 2:27), the choice of Zadok (1 Kgs 2:35), and the relegation of the country high places to inferior statues (cf. 2:36 with 2 Kgs 23:9).

We need now to observe some of the ways in which this material has been structured literarily. The most obvious matter to be noted is the interweaving of positive and negative elements. On the positive side, we see the emergence of Samuel; the unusual character of his birth, development, and divine calling are detailed. Negatively, we observe the degradation of the priestly house of Eli, and the corrupt practices associated with the religious life of that time. Theologically, we see God at work, raising up new leadership while passing judgment on the existing leaders.

These developments are presented by the narrator in striking fashion. Chapter 1 sets the stage. Here we are presented with a

faithful Israelite, Hannah, whose physical difficulties (barrenness) parallel the religious situation of the time: decadent
leadership with no word from the Lord. At the same time,
Hannah's faithfulness is paralleled by God's continued faithful,
though unobtrusive, activity. Her vow to give any offspring she
might have to the Lord becomes the vehicle through which God
is able to work to bring about renewal in the life of the
community.

The psalm in 2:1-10 provides the theological interpretation of
what God is about in this situation. On the one hand, the theme
of God's judgment on the wicked (including leaders) is
highlighted. This theme is quite well suited to the subsequent
description of the wicked priests (lack of attention to God's
holiness, arrogant, greedy/well-fed, coercive in 2:12-17, 22-25),
and of God's response to it (weighing actions; bringing down
from seats of honor in 2:33; making the well-fed hungry in 2:32,
26; making the house of Eli barren in 2:33-34; killing in 2:33-34;
and taking strength away in 2:31). On the other hand, the theme
of renewal is also made clear. God enables birth for the barren
one, brings new life, raises up the poor and lowly; and
(particularly evident in later Samuel materials, but anticipated in
2:35) he enables the lowly Samuel (in the words of 2:8) to "sit
with princes" and exalts the house of David.

The themes in 2:1-10 of bringing down and raising up, of
creating something out of nothing, and of blessing and presence,
provide an interpretation of God's unobtrusive activity throughout the larger narrative. It is interesting to note that this
interpretation of what God is about in history is rooted in a
theology of creation (2:8b, "for"); God's lifting up of the lowly
and putting down the mighty is in tune with what God is about in
the world, as a whole. Thus, the birth and calling of Samuel is
placed within a cosmic pattern.

● It has been common to ignore the important role of this psalm in
its present context, largely because it was thought to have been
introduced by a redactor (editor) into an older narrative. But,
increasingly, scholarship has seen that the theology of the redactor

needs to be given serious consideration. We have seen how this approach provides a hermeneutical key for understanding the larger narrative. The psalm makes it improbable that the emphasis in any interpretation of these chapters ought to be placed on the negative or polemical, i.e., an anti-Eli piece. Rather, the emphasis is on the new, life-giving work of God in the midst of a negative situation.

Beginning with 2:11*b*, the literary artistry in presenting the theme is especially evident. Basically, this is accomplished by the repetition of a virtual refrain:

2:11*b* —"The boy *ministered* to the *Lord, in the presence* of Eli the priest."

2:18 —"Samuel *was ministering* before the *Lord,* a boy girded with linen ephod."

2:21*b* —The boy Samuel *grew in the presence* of the *Lord.*"

2:26 —"The boy Samuel continued to *grow* in stature and in favor with the *Lord* and men."

3:1*a* —"The boy Samuel *was ministering* to the *Lord* under *Eli.*"

3:19f. —"Samuel *grew,* and the *Lord* was with him, and let none of his words fall to the ground . . . and the word of Samuel came to *all Israel.*"

As one can see, this refrain punctuates the narrative throughout these two chapters. Continuity is provided by the references to Samuel and his faithfulness, as well as to the Lord and his presence; development is seen in the use of growth language, but most particularly in the absence of "ministering" language in the conclusion to chap. 3. The focus of the section seems finally to be found in the Word of God/prophet language of 3:19–4:1.

Interspersed with this refrain are three kinds of material: (a) language describing the corrupt state of the clergy (2:12-17; 2:22-25); (b) statements descriptive of present activity on the part of God and the faithful (2:19-21*a*; 3:1*b*-10; 3:15-18); and (c) prophetic statements regarding the future, reflecting God's response in both negative and positive terms, words of judgment and grace (2:27-36; 3:11-14).

The movement evident in these sections may be described as initially largely negative, with the refrain, and 2:19-21a, serving to note continuity in human faithfulness and in divine graciousness in the midst of corruption. Thus, the prophetic word enters the scene in 2:27 and serves to resolve the negative/positive tension. God will now act, passing judgment on the current leaders and raising up new mediators: a faithful priest (2:35) and a prophet of the Lord (3:20). The prophetic word of judgment is repeated (2:27-36; 3:11-14) as a way of focusing separately on the two new leaders God is preparing.

The initiation of judgment and promise differ at one key point. While judgment assumes a largely future reference, the promise begins to take shape in the present. The call comes to Samuel, and he immediately begins to function as a prophet. Having heard the word of the Lord (3:11-14), he faithfully repeats it to Eli (3:18). The content serves to verify his status as a prophet and his continuity with the "man of God" of 2:27, since Eli (who was addressed in 2:27) saw that the two prophetic oracles had essentially the same content. Thus he could only state, "It is the Lord" (3:18). There is a significant ironic point here. Samuel is prepared for his prophetic calling (and finally recognized) by the very persons he is being called to replace, corrupt and incompetent as they are. Perhaps this is also a testimony to God's working even in the midst of such a travesty.

The conclusion (3:19–4:1) serves to summarize the key concern of the larger unit. Samuel, having been recognized as a prophet by the present leader, is now recognized as such by "all Israel." Moreover, the Lord continues to appear to Samuel, so that the word is no longer rare in Israel (cf. 3:1).

Thus, a new era in the history of Israel has begun. Out of the fires of judgment has emerged a new leadership for the community of faith. God has raised up a prophet who will give a new shape to the future.

- These paragraphs demonstrate the importance of considering the larger context in determining the meaning of any given pericope. For one thing, it would appear that this context disallows any understanding of 3:1-10 as an example-story for youth in the present. This might, in turn, shed some light on the use of this story by the Gospel of Luke: Is Luke suggesting that a new prophetic era has dawned in the person of Jesus?

We now need to focus more precisely on chap. 3, especially vv 1-10. First of all, it might be noted that this chapter contains an outline which is similar to that found in other "call narratives." The structure might be outlined as follows: Divine confrontation (vv 2-10); commission (vv 11-14); objection (v 15); reassurance (vv 16-19*a*); and sign-authentication (3:19*b*–4:1). One can profitably compare these elements with the calls of Moses (Exod 3:1-12), Gideon (Judg 6:11*b*-21), Jeremiah (1:4-10), and Ezekiel (1:1–3:11). Although this narrative differs somewhat from the others, not least in that God (or a divine messenger) is not speaking throughout, there is still a rhythm of thought that indicates that this, too, is a "call narrative."

Chapter 3:1 gives notice that this is an era, oft-repeated in the history of Israel, when God's word was not often revealed. The parallel phrase, "no frequent vision," would normally not have reference to a visual image, but to an event in which words are received and insights gained. The "how" of these communications is left unspoken, though they normally occur at night and are to be distinguished from dreaming. The language is used almost exclusively in prophetic contexts (see Lam 2:9; Ezek 7:26), however. The chapter thus begins and ends with language that focuses on Samuel as a prophet.

- These word-events, or visions, are a difficult matter to interpret. Modern psychological discoveries do not seem to be of assistance. Would a tape recorder have picked up any sound? Are there comparable contemporary experiences? We may be dealing with a phenomenon that is common to our own day. Yet, because our perception of God's involvement in our lives is usually general and remote, we would not attribute our insights to God in the way that Israel did.

While the accent of the narrative is on hearing, it is striking that the visual element is not lacking. God not only speaks, but "stands forth" (3:10). What Samuel might have seen is quite unclear, but there is concreteness to the divine presence that is continuous with other call narratives, and testifies to the fact that, for Israel, the Word of God is usually embodied.

The language of 3:1 could be misleading; it almost seems as if God had decided to be silent. On the contrary, the fourfold appearance in vv 4-10 serves to highlight the deity's perseverance. There is a constant seeking to find one who would speak the Word. Again and again, the call comes.

The larger context also makes it clear that the human situation has a profound effect upon the hearing of the Word of God. Certainly the continued reiterations of the negative human behaviors in chap. 2 provide the context for 3:1. The fact that the sons of Eli had "no regard for the Lord" (2:12) was a changed situation as over against the past (see 2:27-28). The lack of a vision from God is thus certainly due in significant part to the lack of vision in the leaders. The text seems to use the language of blindness in more than a physical sense (see 1:12-14; 3:2; 4:15; cf. 2:29), as also perhaps the language of hearing (2:25b). On the other hand, Samuel is attentive to the ministry to which he is called; he hears and sees.

In addition to stressing perseverance, the fourfold appearance of God is intended to stress the difficulty that the Word of God has in "getting through" in this moment in Israel's life. It is not simply because Samuel is inexperienced, not having previously received such a personal revelation (3:7). Rather, even with all his experience in ministering in the sanctuary where God is believed to be present, he obviously had not even heard of such a possibility. Moreover, Eli, though finally recognizing what is happening, likewise had seemed oblivious to such a possibility.

The repetition also makes the point that the call is from God. All human possibilities are eliminated.

The word which comes to Samuel, and which Samuel in turn gives to Eli, is a typical prophetic word of judgment. Though reluctant to pass the word on, at Eli's prompting the lad tells everything. Eli immediately recognizes it as a Word of the Lord. Samuel is thus recognized by the present religious leaders of Israel as one who speaks the Word of the Lord. God has made a new beginning with Israel.

The change from v 1 to vv 19ff. is indeed a massive one. We move from the "boy Samuel" to a mature individual; from one who is ministering "under Eli" to one who is the prophetic leader for "all Israel"; from a rare Word of God to one which is abundant. No longer is there merely a "no good report that I hear the people of the Lord spreading abroad" (2:24); the Word of the Lord comes to all Israel through Samuel. He is established as a prophet, and his priestly responsibilities are no longer in focus.

While the promise regarding a faithful priest still stands, vv 19ff. push Shiloh and its priesthood into the background while lifting up the word of the prophet. Shiloh is no longer important as a cultic/priestly center, but as a place where the Word of God is revealed to the prophet (v 21). Given the events to follow in chaps. 4–6, the necessity for this becomes apparent. With the destruction of Shiloh and its sanctuary, and the loss of the focus of God's presence (the ark), the word of the prophet becomes the sole point of continuity for the presence of God in the midst of the people.

> ● The evident importance of leadership here seems to be applicable in any age. The degree to which God has chosen to be dependent upon good leadership in the spreading abroad of the Word is striking. While the Word of God certainly is prior to any human response, and while it is creative in the effects it has upon the community of faith (raising up those who are nothing to become something), the importance of human response in the articulation of that Word cannot be diminished. It is through leaders like Samuel that the Word can indeed reach all Israel.

We return to the word that the exiles would have heard in this text. A number of parallels between the situation of the text, and their own, would have been evident to them. (That such parallels were being drawn at that time is clear from Jer 7:12.) They could look back on their recent history in the land and see a succession of corrupt leaders (though the figure of Eli would represent more ineptness than corruption, it would appear), leaders who were not enabling the Word of God to get through to the people of faith. At the same time, the loss of the ark and the destruction of Shiloh (see 1 Samuel 4–6) would parallel the loss of Jerusalem and the temple in their own time. With such a recent history, the people were looking at the apparent end of both the Word of God and the presence of God.

God's raising up of Samuel in the midst of such a time would have been a highly reassuring word for them. The problem is not that God, even in the midst of just judgment, has determined to be silent. The deity is always and perseveringly at work, calling those who would speak the Word to the people. As God in the past has raised up such leaders, so it could happen again. The word of the prophet becomes the point of continuity for the presence of God. Or, even more to the point, this has already happened. Prophets like Jeremiah and Ezekiel have been raised up by God in more recent days. It is true that, also like Samuel, they have had harsh words of judgment to speak to the people (see Jer 7:12), but their words have been authenticated in their own time—the Lord has not let any of their words fall to the ground.

At the same time, the calling of Samuel is used to paint a larger canvas, largely through the interpretation provided by the psalm in 1 Sam 2:1-10. God's raising up of the lowly Samuel to sit with princes is seen to be a paradigm of the way in which God works in the world. This would have been an important word for the exiles, a word that assures them that, even in their low estate, God is at work to bring life out of barrenness.

> • Even in this latter point, we see that the implications of this text for today are not in terms of an example-story. It does not speak of what the people of God ought to be or do; it speaks of what God did in a time when they were being wrenched out of familiar religious patterns and when future possibilities were not clear.

Both a general, and specific, reference can be drawn for people of God in such dire straits today. Generally, given the psalm in chap. 2, it becomes a word about God's priorities: siding with the distressed, the lowly, the needy, and working to raise them to wholeness and life. This entails judgment upon the corrupt, the oppressors, and the tyrants. The raising up of Samuel from barrenness to growth and stature is an indication of what God is about among the faithful for whom life has been diminished. Inasmuch as "growth" is associated with God's creative activity, and is unobtrusive (it is not obvious that God is so involved), this would be an indication of the way in which God is often involved in the life of the people.

Specifically, it speaks of God's concern for raising up leaders for the community of faith and of perseverance in calling them. Thus, Samuel's response (3:10) is not an example-word for all the people of God, for only a few are called to be Samuels. Lifting up Samuel's response to this calling should be cast in such terms as: In any community of faith there may be one or more persons whom God is calling to serve as special mediators, so all need to examine themselves to see whether they are the ones who should be listening. But, to cast this text in terms of "the priesthood of all believers" is not being true to the concerns of the passage; only a calling to the ministry of the Word is being addressed.

An Unconditional Promise (2 Samuel 7:1-17)

This is one of the most studied texts in the deuteronomic history. There are numerous reasons why this is so, among them because it has been identified as one of the so-called "messianic" texts so beloved by the people of God. Its appointment as one of the lectionary texts for the Advent season has no doubt heightened its importance for the Christian church in particular. Does this contemporary role correspond to its significance for ancient Israel? Or, have the christological connections tended to distort its meaning?

The fundamental progression of thought in these verses is as follows: David comes to the prophet Nathan out of a concern to build Yahweh a more permanent house (vv 1-2). After an initially positive response, Nathan returns to David with a new word from God, namely, that such a house ought not be built in view of Yahweh's history with the people to this point (vv 3-7). Rather than a concern for a divine house, Yahweh turns the conversation to the establishment of a house for David, which will affect the establishment of the whole people of Israel (vv 8-11*a*). The promise of an eternal dynasty follows, with the special relationship betwen David and Yahweh extended to include the royal descendants: "I will be his father, and he shall be my son." Although individual kings might have to be chastened because of their sin, the promise to the dynasty as a whole would not fail (vv 11*b*-17). After the establishment of the Davidic house, then a concern for Yahweh's house would be in order (v 13*a*).

How this chapter came to be shaped has occasioned numerous scholarly discussions. Only a few comments can be suggested here. The basic observation is that vv 1-7 are concerned with a house for Yahweh, while vv 8-29 are concerned with a house for David (except for v 13*a*). Thus, it has been suggested that two originally distinct concerns have been joined, with the placement of v 13*a* being occasioned by the editorial conflation. Within vv 8-29, vv 11*b*-15 are thought to be the more ancient heart of the promise, while vv 18-29, David's responsive prayer, and vv 8-11*b*, are thought to be later (perhaps deuteronomic) expansions on the basic oracle of promise. The result is that two traditions identified as words of Nathan to David have been brought together, but in uncertain relationship to one another (see below).

This text is part of a larger context that is important to consider, especially its role in the larger deuteronomic history and in this section of 2 Samuel. A solid case can be made for concluding that the promise to David in this chapter constitutes one of the key junctures in the entire history of Israel. Later Israel continued to draw life from this promise, and many thought that her future was finally dependent upon it.

It is striking to note that this tradition is not associated with Samuel's choice of David to be king (see 1 Samuel 16). Rather, it is connected with David's "full-blown" kingship. This may be in

order to give the faithfulness of David a more prominent role.
While this does not mean that the promise is made dependent in
any way upon human endeavor, nonetheless, it is given to a
person of faith. Thus the preceding chapters make it clear that
David has captured Jerusalem and decisively defeated the
Philistines (chap. 5). Moreover, he has rescued the ark and
brought it into his new capital (chap. 6). Because this object
symbolizes the divine rule over Israel, David's act constitutes
Jerusalem as the religious center, and not simply as the political
capital. David is thus seen to have been faithful in making
provision for the place of God among the people of Israel (it is
precisely his concern that is celebrated in Psalm 132, following
which, promises of God are made to the Davidic house). Chapter
7:1 captures all these developments in a single sentence, stressing
that, finally, it is God who has made these events possible.

The relationship between the kingship of Saul and that of
David is also important to consider in this connection. In our
chapter, negative reference is made to the violence of Saul's era
(vv 10-11) and to God's rejection of him (v 15). The closing
narrative of chap. 6 had made it clear that the house of Saul
(embodied in Michal) is being rejected in favor of the Davidic
house (6:16-23). Going back still further, 1 Samuel 8 and 12 had
made it evident that Saul's office had its roots in the sinful desire
of the people for a king. There are no signs in the present chapter
of such an understanding, however. Whereas the kingship of
Saul was the culmination of the sins of the period of the judges, a
kingship which the Lord rejected, the kingship of David
represents the inauguration of a new era in the relationship
between God and the people. Some anticipation of this can be
seen in those texts where Saul and David are contrasted (cf. 1
Sam 13:13-14; 15:28; 20:14-16; 2 Sam 5:2). In David, God is to
make a new beginning with the people of Israel.

Profitable comparisons may be made between Joshua and
David, so that the deuteronomic historian may well have
understood David to be a new Joshua. The language of
servanthood is used of both (Joshua 1; 24; 2 Sam 7:5, 18ff.), as is
the theme of rest from Israel's enemies (Josh 1:13; 21:44; 23:1;

2 Sam 7:1, 11). In David, we find Israel at another crucial juncture in her existence, a moment wherein issues of leadership are paramount. Just as God raised up Joshua for that earlier moment, so now David is raised up for similar leadership of the people.

Into the understanding of kingship, a decisive religious factor has been introduced: the promise of God is bound up with the dynasty in ways which are not true of other kings or dynasties. Although it is made clear in the subsequent narratives that the Davidic kingship is a vulnerable, indeed a blameworthy institution, it has a special role to play in Israel's destiny. In the eyes of the deuteronomic historian, therefore, the only acceptable kings are those of this divinely chosen line. (This perspective has antecedents in Deut 17:15, where the divine election of kings becomes the chief criterion for legitimacy.)

The materials which follow immediately in 2 Samuel 8 appear to be in tension with the statement in 2 Sam 7:1 that God "had given him rest from all his enemies." Now, it does not appear to have been accomplished. Yet, the "rest" spoken of in 7:1 is also spoken of in terms of promise in 7:11. It is not viewed as something to be accomplished once and for all; there is a "now and not yet" character to it. Thus, that chap. 7 is followed with a further list of military accomplishments appears designed to show how the promise of rest is once again brought to fulfillment in the reign of David.

Continued reference to the promises to David are made throughout the deuteronomic history. What has been promised to David is fulfilled in Solomon (1 Kgs 8:15-26). Even though Solomon is not true to the God of David, the promise continues to be articulated, even if more limited in scope (1 Kgs 11:11-13; 32-39). The promise was proclaimed both in the face of continued apostasy on the part of other descendants of David (see 1 Kgs 15:4-6; 2 Kgs 8:19) and in time of faithfulness (see 2 Kgs 18:3-7; 22:2). Claims of divine protection of Jerusalem for the sake of David are also made (2 Kgs 19:34; 20:6). The actualization of the promise plays a role in how the deuteronomic history ends, with its reference to the release of King Jehoiachin

(2 Kgs 25:27ff.). Thus, it is a promise that has decisively shaped Israel's life through times of apostasy and faithfulness, and is finally the historian's only basis for hope for the people in exile.

It has been suggested that certain passages, particularly 1 Kgs 2:4; 8:25; and 9:4-5, make the unconditional promise to David into a conditional one. How are these passages to be related to one another? These exceptional oracles all pertain to Solomon, and may be applicable to the entirety of Israel (i.e., including the northern kingdom), and not to the Davidic throne per se. Thus, in 1 Kgs 11:11-13 and 32-38, we see that the united kingdom is split up because of Solomon's sin, and the throne of "Israel" is given to Jeroboam (at least temporarily—v 39), while the southern kingdom is allowed to be maintained within the Davidic line. Thus, while the articulation of the unconditional promise in the chapters that follow is more limited in scope, given the sins of Solomon, it, nonetheless, stands as the deuteronomic historian's fundamental perspective on the Davidic monarchy. The promise is, finally, dependent only on the faithfulness of God.

It is important to note that the Davidic covenant was not thought to displace or supplement God's covenant with the people as a whole at Mt. Sinai. Through the king, who is the embodiment of the rule of God among the people, the promise to David extends to all (see 2 Sam 5:3). Verses 9-11 in our text clearly indicate the effect of the choice of David upon the entire people: rest for David is rest for all. Verse 24, in David's prayer, explicitly states the promise to the people in language like that used with David (see also 1 Samuel 12). Generally speaking, the establishment of the throne of David forever, implies a people over whom the king rules.

The juxtaposition of concern for temple and dynasty in this chapter has occasioned numerous discussions. At the least, the juxtaposition in and of itself suggests that there was concern about the proper relationship between the two. While political factors may have been at work in the original situation, since a temple was a foreign institution and would have detracted from the establishment of the Davidic monarchy in the eyes of many, the theological perspective given in the text needs to be emphasized: God has traditionally moved about with the people, using a portable sanctuary as a dwelling place. The implication is that if a permanent "house" were built, then God might be thought to be localized, or even confined, and would not be perceived by the community as one whose dwelling place was with the people wherever they happen to be. And yet, permission to build a temple is given a bit later (v 13a), and that event, in fact, occurs. Thus, there is no opposition to the temple per se. (However, 1 Kings 8 carefully guards against interpretations which would localize God.) What is the reason for the delay from the perspective of the historian? First Chronicles 22:8 gives a reason not alluded to in this text. It might be stated as follows: God's promise to David and his dynasty is seen to have priority over any word concerning the temple. The temple is dispensable; God's promise to David is eternal. Given the final exilic shaping of this material (v 10 contains exilic allusions), that would be a very important word to hear: the heart of the promise is not concerned with a place of worship (now destroyed), but with their future as a people in whose midst God will be present wherever they may be.

At the same time, the temple is not an unimportant institution: "He shall build a house for my name" (v 13a). (We have already seen the important role given to the proper worship of Yahweh in the deuteronomic history, especially in the discussion of Joshua 24.) The overriding concern is that the temple be the vehicle for the true worship of Yahweh; all else is subordinate to that.

Deuteronomy 12 provides the theological framework for all discussion about the importance of the temple (cf. also 1 Kings 8). There, provision is made for the establishment of one sanctuary, at a place that God alone will choose. It is this principle (and not a specific location) which is important. Such centralization would safeguard worship so that it not become contaminated with the practices of the Canaanites. This, in fact, had happened at various "country shrines" by the time that Deuteronomy was compiled (8th cent.) and so a radical surgery was advocated: Destroy them all and concentrate worship at a place where its character can be closely watched. What was advocated in Deuteronomy 12 was actually carried out for the first time under King Josiah (cf. 2 Kings 22–23). The historian justifies this action by including numerous comments about the idolatry that has occurred at other sanctuaries prior to this (cf. 1 Kgs 12:26-33; 18:17-22). In fact, it was precisely for this reason that Israel, the northern kingdom, had stumbled to her death (2 Kgs 17:7-18).

It can be said without equivocation that there was finally only one matter that made for the life or death of Israel, and that was faithfulness to God. Or, to use the language of the first commandment: "You shall have no other gods before me." And, it was the area of worship which provided the litmus test for determination of whether the king or the people were loyal to Yahweh or not. This radical step of a single sanctuary had to be promoted because history had demonstrated that true worship could not be safeguarded, and a unity of belief and practice assured, if there were many different places for worship.

> • The reluctance displayed in our text for building the temple is an important consideration for discussion in any community of faith, since human nature seems unchanging at this point. It is not uncommon for people to conceive of the sanctuary in terms of a "House of God," as a place where God has, in some sense, taken up residence. Thus, it is an easy transition to an understanding which views the sanctuary as the only place where God is really present among the people. To localize or confine God in this fashion is in effect to deny a comparable presence elsewhere in daily life.

The text affirms that God has been moving about with the people wherever they are, and when the temple is built it must not be understood as a restriction of the divine presence (cf. 1 Kgs 8:27). Yet, even when God moved about with the people, there was a central place for worship.

> • The utility of a sanctuary, then and now, ought not be dismissed, as if a place "under any green tree" would do. This is true for at least three reasons. (a) A sanctuary brings *order* to the worship of God. An undifferentiated proliferation leads to a lack of discipline

and focus. This can lead all too easily to a perspective that "anything goes," which in Israel made for idolatry, pure and simple. While centralization is (and probably was) unrealistic, the concern for order and discipline is an admirable, and indeed essential, element in the maintenance of true worship. (b) The sanctuary provides a *tangible* aspect for the divine presence. God's people, in their humanity, have a need for concreteness in their relationship with God; a purely spiritual relationship is incomplete. Thus, in the provision for a dwelling place on earth, God condescends to the human need for the tangible. (c) The sanctuary provides a point of *assurance* of the divine presence. That is, God has promised to be present at a given place, and the people can be confident that they will experience God there, and that all their supplications will be heard (see 1 Kgs 8:28ff.).

The relationship between king and temple is shown throughout the history in the concern that the former is to have for the latter (cf. esp. 1 Kings 8). Again and again, the editor will give an evaluative judgment on the basis of what a king has done in the area of worship (negatively, see 1 Kgs 12:25-33 and the role of Jeroboam; positively, see 2 Kings 22–23 and the role of Josiah). The integral role of prayer in kingship/temple texts (see 2 Sam 7:18-29; 1 Kgs 8:22-53) also indicates something of what was expected of the king in the area of worship.

Something of the argument of vv 8-17 now needs to be explored.

The history of God with David (vv 8-9*a*). Three matters are isolated: God's choice of David to be a prince ("prince" is used, rather than "king," to stress continuities with the period of the judges, and not identification with kings in the ancient Near East); God's presence with David wherever he has gone ("with you" is emphasized in the text); and God's enabling victory over Israel's enemies. This provides the *theological* foundation for the promise that is about to be stated. That is, it is God's electing and saving activity which lies at the basis of the promise, not David's heroic efforts. In fact, the obscure origins of David among the sheepfolds is stressed so that the gracious activity of God stands out all the more. Thus, all talk about the future is based on what

God has done in the past. The God who makes promises is the God who has already acted in decisive, salvific ways on behalf of the one to whom the promise is given. Thus, the promise is not something that is *radically* new; there is an element of newness, but it stands in decisive continuity with what God has already done.

The promises to David (vv 9b-16). The promises which follow are not narrowly associated with the man, David, as we have seen. There is an interweaving of promises to David and the people; their futures are inextricably linked with one another in the promises of God. The ties between these promises, and the promise to Abraham are striking (cf. Gen 12:1-3; 15-18): name, land, blessing, and no more disturbance from enemies round about. The promises to Abraham are believed to be continued in the promises to David (cf. also Joshua 1).

The promise to David, the individual (v 9b). David is promised a great name (cf. 8:13). While the emphasis in the passage, as a whole, is on God's greatness and activity on behalf of the people, the "limelight," as it were, is shared with the king. Yet, finally (as with Josh 3:7), the purpose is not to put David on an equal plane with God, but to witness to the God who works in and through him (see vv 25-26).

The promise to the people (vv 10-11a). As we have noted, the language here echoes the situation in which the exiles found themselves. A survey of prophetic passages, particularly Jeremiah (cf. 23:5-6; 24:5-6; 29:14; 32:37-41; see also Ps 80:8ff.; Ezek 19:10-14), indicates that the language of "place," "planting," and "dwelling securely in their own land," pervades the hope articulated to the exiles. Though this passage probably did not have the exiles in view in its original formulation, it is apparent that it provided a rich resource for later prophetic, and deuteronomic hopes. Hence, the exiles would have read this passage in that light, and seen its promise as applying to them.

It is to be noted that, unlike some of the prophetic passages cited, this text makes no mention of a particular land—only a "place." A number of things are noted about this "place." It is a gift from God; God is the one who will "appoint a place." It is not something which is to be grasped for, but received from the hand of God. The promise is not of a temporary place; it is given for taking root and growing up; it is a place which one will be able to call "home." And, it is a place in which they can dwell securely, free from the roaming and ravaging of violent persons (unlike the situation prevailing throughout the period up to this point). And they shall be given rest—again, a gift of God, not their own achievement. And such a rest is not a static sleeping, but an active well-being.

● The promise of a place is problematic in today's refugee-filled world. Landlessness seems endemic among so many of the world's poor. Is this a promise that applies to them? It is difficult to argue from a promise given to the chosen people to a general promise for all God's creatures. Yet, inasmuch as the promise given to Abraham is intended to become a vehicle for the extension of blessing to all (see Gen 12:1-3), and inasmuch as the Davidic king was promised worldwide dominion and was to bring deliverance to all the poor and needy (Psalm 72), a claim can be made that God's intention for *all* creatures is a place where they can dwell at home and in peace. What God desires for the chosen people is desired for all.

It would be improper to spiritualize this text in such a way as to suggest: Whereas God once desired a land for the people, such is the case no longer. This is often a way for landowners to justify their lack of concern for the landless. Given the nature of human beings, matters of place and space are integral to well-being. Thus, the promises of texts like this must remain grounded in the worldly and the earthly: God's promises are not only oriented to spiritual matters; they include a place one can call home.

Nevertheless, there is a problem. How specific does the promise of the text remain? Does it include the land of Palestine for modern-day Israel? Within the OT period, the promise of land for Israel was fulfilled, both at the time of Joshua and at the return from exile. Can the promise be extended into the indefinite future? The general reference to "place" in this text may point us in the right direction (recognizing that the relationship of modern Jews to the land of Palestine is no simple matter). It is a promise of place, not a specific place. Thus, it would appear that all who are the bearers of such a promise are to work toward a place in peace for all.

The promise to the house of David (vv 11b-16). It is important to note the movement through these verses. Verse 11b begins with a general statement about David's "house," i.e., dynasty. Then, the focus shifts to the first member of the Davidic line, namely, Solomon, "Your son . . . who shall come forth from your body" (cf. 1 Kgs 8:19). God will establish his kingdom (cf. 1 Kgs 2:12), and he will build the temple. Then, the movement shifts back to the dynasty, i.e., "the *throne* of his kingdom *forever*" (v 13b). Verses 14-15 would seem to have specific reference only to Solomon, but inasmuch as they stand between the general reference to throne in v 13b, and the entire dynasty in v 16, they may refer to each king of the Davidic line. Thus, there is an interweaving of the individual and the corporate in these verses, with the corporate as the more prominent.

Once again it is to be noted that the stress is upon what God has done or will do. It is the Lord who declares, who will make the house of David what it is to be (v 11b), and who will raise up the son of David (when David has died, and hence is not able to do it himself) and establish the kingdom. God will be a father to the king and hence relate to him as a son; love for him will continue, even though he is chastened. The decisive action regarding the Davidic dynasty is, thus, seen to be God's own work.

The language of "father" and "son" is very important for our understanding of this passage. The primary usage of this language in the OT, and in the deuteronomic material in particular, is with reference to Israel (Deut 1:31; 8:5; 14:1). These passages are especially instructive, because they refer both to the care which God shows to "sons" (1:31), as well as to the "discipline" which Israel, the "son," experiences at the hand of the father (8:5). Thus, the kings will have the same relationship to God that is enjoyed by the people as a whole (cf. the variety of parental images in Deuteronomy 32).

The father/son language with reference to the Davidic king is elsewhere developed in special ways. This is particularly evident in the royal psalms (see Ps 2:7; 72:1; 89:26-37). Psalm 89 especially develops themes to be found here, and stresses the language of covenant (vv 3-4; cf. 2 Sam 23:5). The covenant is defined essentially as the variety of promises which are given by God to the Davidic line.

Needing special attention is the reference to "steadfast love" (v 15). It sounds as if God's love is something that may be turned on and off, but that it will continue to David in a way that it did not to Saul. However, it is important to note that this is not a general reference to God's love for all creatures. Psalm 89 can help us here: vv 1, 28, and 33 place "steadfast love" in parallel with "covenant" and "faithfulness." Thus, it has reference to something like covenant loyalty. The covenant with David is set apart from that with Saul by being made an everlasting covenant, one which will never fail regardless of how members of the Davidic line might comport themselves.

The connections with Psalm 89 also help point the way to how these verses were understood in an exilic context. It continues to affirm the unconditional promises to David at a time when the people seem to have been forsaken by God. The psalm ends on a questioning note, with a general statement that scorn has been heaped upon the Lord's anointed. The future is open-ended, but the promise continues to be affirmed. In combination with 2 Kgs 25:27-30, 2 Samuel 7 may be said to function in a comparable way. The unconditional promise is stated, but the shape of the future remains uncertain. (Cf. also the relationship between Lam 3:22-33, which has a strong statement about the never ending love of God in midst of chastisement, with the uncertainty of the ending in 5:20-22; cf. also the short ending of the Gospel of Mark.)

Such was the situation in which the exiles found themselves. They hear and believe these promises of God. Throughout the deuteronomic history, from Joshua 1 on, God is revealed as a promise-keeper. The word comes through again and again: God will never break the covenant; God will not fail them or forsake them wherever they might go. Just as the word of the prophets regarding judgment had come to pass again and again, so this word of the prophet Nathan would also come to pass, for God's faithfulness is forever (note that "forever" occurs eight times in this chapter). It is clear, given sin, that there will be judgment (as it was with David so it would be with the people), but to use the words of Ps 30:5 [Hebrew v 6], "His anger is but for a moment, and his favor is for a lifetime." This combination of judgment and enduring promise is exactly in tune with passages in the exilic Deutero–Isaiah (e.g., Isa 54:7-10). And Isa 55:3, with its insistence that the promise to David is a promise to the people, shows how the exiles would have understood 2 Samuel 7. Thus understood, 2 Samuel 7 gave an interpretive key to the exile as a time of chastisement without annihilation, as a moment of death which did not finally negate the promise. Yet, for the exiles, the shape of the future was not yet clear; it was not yet evident how the God who keeps promises will do the keeping. Jehoiachin had been released from prison (2 Kgs 25:27ff.), but the significance of that is yet to be seen. Meanwhile, they are to seek the Lord (Isa 55:6; Lam 3:25; Deut 4:29) and repent (Isa 55:7; 1 Kgs 8:28ff.), which is possible and effective only because God is the faithful one whose promise is at work in their lives. God's promise to David, which is a promise to the people, will not fail. Of that they can be sure.

> ● A significant point of entry into this text for today may be to parallel the variety of exile-like situations faced by the people of God with those of ancient Israel. Just as the promise to David and Israel prevailed through events that made for death, making repentance and a new life possible even though the future was quite unclear, so also it is the promise of God embodied in another son of Jesse, Jesus of Nazareth, which enables Christians to endure their exiles and set their sights on a certain, but yet unshaped, future.

A full discussion of the significance of the Davidic covenant is not possible here. Suffice it to say that a number of royal psalms, particularly 2, 72, 89, and 110, show that the unconditional promise to David came to have a very important place in Israel's thinking about herself and her future. Inasmuch as the king was considered to be the embodiment of the people, the covenant with the king was considered to be a new commitment of God to the people (such as we have seen articulated in Judg 2:1). The essential contents of the covenant promises were the great benefits which would come to the people in and through the reign of the king. Israelite kingship was thus viewed fundamentally as a religious institution. Having been endowed by the Spirit of God at his anointing (in Hebrew, "anointed one"-messiah, cf. 1 Samuel 16), and adopted by God as a son (Ps 2:7), the king was to serve as the earthly representative of God's righteous rule. The king was considered to be the bearer of God's own purposes and goals and, thus, was considered a vehicle for the establishing of God's kingdom in the world. The purpose of each king in his reign, then, was to reach out toward those goals toward which God was working. He was responsible for ruling the people as God would rule them. When the king failed, as he often did, it had disastrous effects upon the entire society (and thus we see why the deuteronomic historian is so hard on the kings in his assessment of them).

Did not history, through the Exile, contradict this promise (of God) to David? Psalm 89 may well be a lament focusing on this question in that context. The prophets, however, had prepared the way for just such a time. It had become clear that the ideal Davidic kingship was not being realized. And yet, it was believed that no king could frustrate the purposes of God. Although the current member of the Davidic line might be a hopeless case, prophets (e.g., Isaiah 9, 11; Jeremiah 23) envisioned a return to kingship as God intended it to be. While such prophets no doubt had reference to one of the very next kings in line, eventually fulfillment was pushed more and more into the future. Someday . . . God would raise up a king, a Messiah. The royal psalms are eventually given this messianic interpretation, and no doubt 2 Samuel 7 (picked up and repeated in the post-exilic books of Chronicles, cf. 1 Chronicles 17) was given such a futuristic interpretation as well.

• Is it legitimate to make a connection between this text and the advent of Jesus? The NT makes this affirmation (cf. Luke 1:68ff.), but one ought not say that the author of 2 Samuel 7 had the Messiah, or Jesus, in mind when he wrote what he did. It is, of course, a matter of faith, and not exegetical argumentation, which enables one to confess that Jesus fulfills the promise of God articulated there.

You Are the Man (2 Samuel 12:1-15)

The David/Bathsheba affair, followed by Nathan's "You are the man!" speech, has long captured the attention of young and old alike. More often than not, the story has been used as a way of zeroing in on the adultery commandment. Is this a proper use of this story, or must we look elsewhere for the heart of the matter?

We must, first of all, briefly consider the larger context of which this text is a part. The narrative sequence, 2 Samuel 9–20, 1 Kings 1–12, has long been isolated as an originally independent composition, detailing the reign of David.

There are three primary issues being raised these days regarding this unit:

(1) It has long been called the Succession Narrative, because of an apparent special concern for the question: Who shall succeed David? More recently it has been suggested that there are other more (or just as) prominent concerns reflected therein. For now, it may be best to steer clear of the supposition of any narrow interest on the part of the narrator, and treat the whole as dealing with various aspects of the reign of David.

(2) It has been commonly thought that this material is an example of OT history writing at its best, not least because of its realism and sparse references to divine activity. This assessment has now been revised, so that the material is more accurately to be designated as a story, or historical novel. See especially the large blocks of material that are anecdotal and descriptive of quite private conversations and activities, of which our text is an example.

(3) The independence of the narrative has also been

questioned, and a number of attempts have been made to relate it to other material about David. Nonetheless, whatever form this narrative may have had early in the history of its transmission, it has now been thoroughly integrated by redactors into a larger whole. One significant level of redaction is that of the deuteronomic historian, whose impact may be seen particularly in vv 7-12 of our text.

A smaller context that should be considered is chaps. 10–12. A narrative, largely concerned with the David/Bathsheba affair and its aftermath, is framed by descriptions of the Ammonite war (10:1–11:1 and 12:26-31). Thus, a public, national undertaking provides the immediate context for a private, individual matter. It would appear that we are, thereby, called upon to explore the complex relationship between David's private life and the public order. We will attend to this below.

Within the report of the private episode, our text falls between a description of David's adultery and consequent murder of Uriah, on the one hand (11:2-27), and the aftermath of Nathan's judgment, on the other (12:16-25). On the whole, the movement is from the negative (the adultery) to the positive (the birth of Solomon, beloved of Yahweh). We must now see how our text functions within this narrow context.

First of all, we need to consider Nathan's parable. The parable might be more closely defined as a judgment-eliciting parable. It is told for the specific purpose of eliciting from David an evaluative response so that the Word of God can be heard more pointedly. But, the parable does not have a lesson in itself; it makes a point only if David responds in a certain way. Thus, the parable would not have "worked" if David had responded: "We must have the courts look into this!" (See 2 Samuel 14 for a similar narrative.)

It is likely that, given his response, David perceives that Nathan was talking about a real life situation, and not a fictional one. It is unlikely, however, that an actual legal case was being described; Nathan would not be expected to convey that sort of problem to the king for judgment. There is no indication that Nathan seeks David's counsel regarding the matter of the story.

Rather, there is a typical prophetic abruptness about the entire scene.

What are the characteristics of the parable that enabled it to work? It was not immediately apparent to David how Nathan intended to use the parable; his suspicions were not raised. Yet, it was close enough to David's actual situation so that David could see the parallels, indeed could not escape the force of its implications when Nathan gave the clue. The use of an animal rather than a person is probably the basic element that enabled the guise to work.

In order for the parable to work, it also had to be told in such a way that Nathan could be reasonably sure of the right response from David. This seems to be accomplished in a number of ways: (1) Elements that raise the emotional involvement of the hearer. This is accomplished largely through the description of the relationship between the poor man and the lamb. Verse 3 describes an increasingly intimate relationship between the two, so that finally it becomes like a (the only!) daughter to him, virtually a member of the (motherless!) family. The fact that it is a poor man, and that he has "nothing" but this lamb, and that the antagonist is a rich man, and the guest is a stranger, would all raise the emotional investment. (2) An element of surprise: the expectation is that the rich man (a neighbor!) would take from his own herds rather than take the lamb of someone else. (3) There has to be some similarity between David's personal/moral values and the reprehensibility of the rich man's actions. The positive thing about David's response is that it shows that he has a deep sense of justice. (4) The timing relative to the personal situation of David. The placement of this narrative immediately following chap. 11 may suggest that David is to be understood as suspecting why Nathan is paying him a visit. David's immediate and vehement response in vv 5-6 would thus indicate an over-eagerness to please Nathan, and may reflect his relief that the object of the prophet's anger is someone else.

What issue does the parable raise for David? How does he understand it? This is important for determining the point the parable seeks to make. (It is important to note that, because the parable is not a comparison, detailed correspondence between it and David's situation need not be looked for.) David judges the rich man sharply and announces two verdicts: he deserves to die, and he is to restore the lamb fourfold. The double verdict is due to the fact that the lamb has been shown to be both family member and property. Thus, both killing (for which the death penalty is called for) and stealing (for which restitution is in order) are in view.

David then goes on to give a double reason for his verdict: the act was committed, and no pity was shown (i.e., the man was merciless, without compassion). Again, this indicates that more than theft is in view for David. Not having pity focuses on the personal effect on the poor man (losing a member of the family) and on the attitude of the rich man in the situation. This pushes the matter to the larger issues of justice. This is reinforced by the use of the poor man/rich man contrast. If just stealing, even both stealing and killing, were the only point of the parable, then this contrast would have no special relevance to David's situation. Thus, the larger issue of oppressive power is brought into play. The rich man has failed to honor very basic human relationships; it is not an economic issue at the heart of things. It is interesting to note that the issue of adultery is not in view, nor anything that could be said to be parallel to it.

This interpretation is reinforced by noting the nature of Nathan's accusation and judgment (similar to other prophetic words, cf. Isa. 1:21-25). Some structural items need attention:

12:7	—God delivers David	12:8	—God gives David wives
12:9	—David despises God and murders Uriah	12:10b	—David despises God and takes Uriah's wife
12:10a	—Sword will come to David's house	12:11-12	—Others will take David's wives

First of all, it is to be noted that God's gracious acts on behalf of David are cited as the basis of the accusation, not the law (vv 7-8). It is a matter of rebellion against grace, not disobedience of the commandments, that lies at the heart of the matter for Nathan. God has already given David many things and David's response is to take from others; so now it is God who will take away. This is supported by the fourfold reference to displeasing/ despising the Lord, which both frames this narrative (11:27; 12:14) and prefaces each of the accusations (12:9; 12:10b). This places David's relationship with God, and his flaunting of that relationship, at the center of the issue, not David's being measured over against an external ordinance. David's confession is continuous with this: "I have sinned against the Lord"; it is not, "I have disobeyed the commandments." This is reminiscent of other prophetic approaches to human sin, e.g., "You only have I known of all the families of the earth; therefore I will punish you for your iniquities" (Amos 3:2). But it is especially in line with the deuteronomic understanding of the ethical life: it is to be grounded in what God has done, and to flow naturally from the resultant relationship (see Deut 10:12-22). Nathan thus brings David face to face with God; he cannot escape. Upon David's confession, Nathan's response is the word of forgiveness, without any reference to David's obedience of the law in the future. God has now once again acted graciously on David's behalf, and response to such action should be the sole motivation for David's life.

Second, after his opening statement regarding God's gracious acts, Nathan moves to his twofold accusation and judgment. It is striking that the act of adultery in itself is not lifted up for special attention. The language of adultery is not used (such as is used, e.g., in the Sixth Commandment), nor the language of sexuality. Bathsheba is never mentioned by name; she is always spoken of as the wife of Uriah, or "his wife." The emphasis is on what has been done to Uriah, not to Bathsheba. The sin of adultery is thus painted in terms of other sins—the sin of theft, e.g.. And yet, as we have noted in the parable, it is not an economic issue that is foremost in Nathan's mind, but a failure to honor the most basic of human relationships, which is equal to despising God. Issues of oppressive power also seem to be present here, as in the parable. David, as the man of power, has used that power in oppressive and unjust ways.

> • It has been tempting through the years to make this story into a moral tract, which is concerned with isolating the wrongness of certain specific deeds (adultery, murder). Thus, one would emerge from the story with the following truths: Do not kill; do not commit adultery. And hence, in any contemporary use of the story, comparable truths would need to be stated. But the language used in the story, as well as the larger context, suggest broader concerns to the modern interpreter. It is not specific sins that are in view, but sin as committed by those who have power over the lives of others. But even more, as we shall see, there is a concern about the effects of such sin, about forgiveness that is available even for the worst of sinners, and about the activity of God that works in, with, and under all human affairs.

Next, we need to take a closer look at the specific judgments which Nathan pronounces: the sword will come to David's house (v 10a) and the raising up of evil from within, which is to take the form of his own wives being ravished. Thus, the judgments come in the same form as the sins which set the judgments in motion: murder and adultery. "The punishment fits the crime."

It is important to note that the judgments announced in v 10a and vv 11-12 are fulfilled in the later chapters concerning the history of David. We have seen this to be an important theme in the historian's theological perspective. The violent and adulterous activity of the house of David is returned to again and again. The violence is seen particularly in the deaths of David's sons, Amnon, Absalom, and Adonijah (2 Sam 13:18; 1 Kings 2), and the adultery in the actions of Amnon (2 Sam 13:8ff.), but especially Absalom (16:22).

> • One of the difficulties for the interpreter here, particularly in the correlation of v 11b and 16:22, is to decide whether Nathan's original announcement about the future was so precise, or whether

later editors, in view of their knowledge of what had actually happened, gave greater specificity to Nathan's word than was originally the case. It is impossible to decide this in any final way. It is possible that v 11a (which like v 10a is a more general statement) was the original oracle to which v 11b-12 was added in the light of what happened later. Thus, it would be an editor's way of making sure that the connection between the oracle of judgment and the fulfillment not be missed by the reader. This would not necessarily deny that Nathan *could* have been so specific. In either case, there was, indeed, a fulfillment of the word of the prophet and (like many other instances in the OT) the amount of specific correspondence between prophecy and fulfillment is beside the point. In either case, only faith can discern such connections.

This raises questions about God as well. Did not God occasion evil events in the world worse than those against which the judgment was originally spoken? Was there not a compounding of the same sins which were to be judged? Instead of one instance of adultery, it was multiplied; instead of one murder, there were many. Moreover, what kind of justice is there in this? It is not "an eye for an eye" justice; it is many eyes for one.

● One needs to use great care here lest God come off in ways quite unintended by the text and which reinforce certain common misconceptions about the OT God. It is not that God announces judgment in order to bring effects of the sin into being in some direct fashion. The sin will have disastrous effects apart from the word announced by Nathan. Nor does the announcement of judgment mean that there will now be different effects of sin as over against what would be the case if there were no announcement. By connecting the judgment to God, the prophet does two things: (a) He makes the sin-judgment connection inescapable to David; it is, in fact, his sin that will make for all this disaster. This, then, becomes a part of Nathan's intent to convict David for what he has done, to bring about repentance and, hence, introduce good effects into the future to counteract the evil. (b) At the same time, God is not uninvolved in the aftermath of David's sin. It is a part of the order of the world that sin will have such effects, and that order will continue to be maintained (here God is seen to be more directly involved in the maintenance of the structures of the world than we are commonly prepared to admit today). At the same time, as we shall see, God is also involved in such a way to bring about good in the midst of the disaster.

One further note needs to be made about the judgment. Sins committed by the powerful always have greater evil effects on society than sins by others. David's sin, like the sin of all kings (note here esp. the judgments made concerning kings throughout the deuteronomic history), will have repercussions, not only for his own family, but also for the future of Israel. These private sins of David will have public effects. There is a sense then in which this event explains much of what is to follow, including the accession of Solomon to the throne (note that intrigue, deceit, and murder are repeated at that point in the narrative, 1 Kings 1–2).

● A warning is necessary here: one should not apply this text in any easy fashion to all individuals. It has centrally to do with those who are in leadership positions, and whose sins are especially havoc-provoking. Yet, in some sense, the Davidic king is the embodiment of all Israel, and the picture of sin, accusation, judgment, and forgiveness exhibit a common pattern among the people of God.

David's response to this accusation and judgment speech is, "I have sinned against the Lord." Such repentance, just like the judgment, has an effect beyond the person of David. While it serves to ameliorate the effects of judgment on his own situation, it also has more far-reaching ramifications upon the history which is to follow. The effects of repentance/forgiveness work against the effects of sin, so that the future will not be quite the disaster it otherwise would have been.

The immediate effects of David's confession are both striking and puzzling. Nathan assures him of the forgiveness of God, and that death will not be visited upon him personally. Actually, in Nathan's announcement of judgment there was no specific word about David's own death, only words about his family (vv 10a,

11*a*), though one could perhaps infer that it might well have been forthcoming given the accusation of murder (Lev 24:17) and adultery (Deut 22:22). In any case, David will not die, but the child of the illicit union will. The amelioration of the judgment, you will note, applies only to David himself; the judgments announced in vv 10-12 are not ameliorated at all.

One of the interpretive difficulties in this verse is the harshness of the fact that a child will die instead of David. This is in tune with a long-standing tradition regarding the visitation of the sins of the fathers upon the children (cf. Exod 20:5), an idea which appears to be denied by Ezek 18:20 (cf. Deut 24:16). The latter passages are not really applicable in this instance, however. They have reference to specific legal (Deuteronomy) or spiritual/ historical (Ezekiel) situations. Our passage has reference to inevitable "snowballing" effects that David's sin will have upon his own family. God's striking the child sick (v 15) is likely an interpretation subsequent to the event that is placed back upon it. The child of the union did become sick and die. The community asks: "How is one to understand this death?" It is then explained in terms of the effects of David's sinfulness.

● One should be careful in any use to which this text might be put. It is an age-old question, which is voiced so pointedly in John 9:2, "Who sinned, this man or his parents, that he was born blind?" Sometimes explicit connections can be made between the sin of parents and the health of their children (e.g., the pregnant mother taking drugs). At other times, no such connection can be made at the individual level; but it could at the social level. One might, for example, appeal to the sin of the larger community which built a nuclear plant whose leaking radiation affected the health of the children born in the neighborhood. If the author of our narrative were to speak of the sickness of these children, he would speak in terms of the judgment of God upon those who made such sickness possible. Not that God caused the sickness, but that the structures of the world, which continue to be maintained by God, are such that sins will have such effects. There are still other times when the connection between the sin and the sickness is not possible to determine (e.g., in our narrative, or today, "crib deaths"). Nonetheless, the biblical narrator will assume that God is not removed from the moral order and, hence, will speak of a divine involvement here, as well.

It is clear from what follows (particularly v 22) that it was not a foregone conclusion that the child would die; David believed that his prayers might well be effective in turning the child from sickness to health. It is clear from 2 Kgs 20:1-7 that a prophet's word about the future can be turned around and not come to fulfillment because of the prayers of those involved. This means that there is no rigid retributionary system at work here; human actions have the capacity to deflect the effects of sin in one way or another. It is, however, never certain what effect they might have ("Who knows?" v 22).

This may be the appropriate time to go back over the story once again, only this time from the point of view of Nathan. While this is the story of David, it is also the story of a prophet of the Word of God. It is the prophet's story which provides a crucial counterpoint.

Nathan's role in the story may be outlined as follows:

1. *Prophetic vigilance.* This entails discernment of the situation of the people of God. Nathan is alert to what is going on in royal circles, and moves in where a word of God needs to be heard.

2. *Prophetic wisdom.* It is not enough for the prophet to be discerning. The prophet must also know how to shape a word for just this situation or that, so that the word of God will strike home. In this situation, Nathan picks a parable as the most helpful vehicle. It is replete with wisdom, as we have seen.

3. *Prophetic boldness.* Given the status of David, considerable courage was necessary to confront him and announce boldly: "You are the man!"

4. *Prophetic proclamation of forgiveness.* Even with the most heinous of sins committed, with the harshest of judgments announced, there is still room for repentance; there is room for change that makes for good. And at that response from David, the prophet proclaims: "The Lord has put away your sin; you shall not die."

Overall, the actions and words of the prophet provide a crucial turning point in the story of David. It needs to be said clearly that the role he plays is fundamentally a gracious one. Without his entrance onto the scene, there would have been no clarity introduced into what was happening in Israel's history, particularly with respect to God's relationship to what is occurring. On the one hand, he makes clear (what the narrator also makes clear) that what has happened is displeasing to God (note again: it is the despising of God and not the disobedience of commandments that provides the focus). This intervention enables the movement to repentance in David. On the other hand, Nathan announces not only the judging work of God but also the saving work of God. Indeed, judgment is undertaken precisely so that positive effects might be forthcoming.

Thus, this text provides a fundamental interpretive clue for the entire story of David. God has been, and will continue to be, at work behind the scenes, seeking to achieve a purpose. Indeed, not only behind the scenes, for here the prophet is sent to be quite explicit regarding what the word of God is for the moment. This explicitness stands in some tension with the emphatic hiddenness that is evident elsewhere in the larger narrative, and hence we might conclude that they were originally separate literary pieces. Yet, it needs also to be said that this tension manifests a theological dialectic which is sophisticated, indeed. This chapter is comparable to other revelations in seemingly secular contexts. For example, the revelation to Moses at the burning bush is a laser-beam-like moment in the midst of a long history of divine hiddenness; and it is just this moment that illumines all that happens subsequent to it. So also here, the prophetic moment serves as a key to understanding what is to follow. The hiddenness of God is not abandonment by God; the prophetic moments clarify what God is indeed doing behind the scenes. And even more, the future will be different because of this explicit involvement of the prophet. He not only makes the situation clear; he shapes the future.

At the same time, the actions of the human beings involved are not immaterial. What people do counts; their actions make a difference not only as far as the human situation is concerned, but as far as the course of the divine working is concerned. It matters that David repents; it matters not only for David but for Israel, especially given his important leadership role.

It is this positive response by David that, finally, provides the force of the narrative from the human side, and not his sins of adultery and murder. This is shown, above all, by the way in which he responds in vv 16-23 and by God's response to the birth of Solomon in vv 24-25. Thus, far from being a narrative which serves to take the monarchy down a notch or two, David finally emerges as an exemplary figure in the repentant way in which he responds to the word of the prophet. David stands in sharp contrast to most of the kings of the later monarchy, and one wonders whether the story might have been intended as an example story for subsequent kings of the Davidic dynasty.

But, above all, the story is a witness to the graciousness of God. Amidst all the evil perpetrated by David, God is at work, bringing about good. And, that goodness is finally a surprise. Out of what might be called the most compromising situation in David's life, the child Solomon, heir to David, is born. "And the Lord loved him" (v 24). What a remarkable statement! Far from holding a grudge against David for all the trouble he had caused, God forgives, forgets, and loves this new child. God is always ready to begin again.

It is this latter angle of vision on the text that needs to be lifted up in any contemporary usage. The text may be used to speak of the frailty of humans and the havoc-wreaking effects that sin can perpetrate. It may also be used to show the importance of human repentance, and the positive effects that it can have for the life of the people of God. But, above all, the text is a witness to divine activity: sending a prophet with a word to bring about changes for good, and responding to a repentant servant with forgiveness, with all the potential for good that such a word has for those to whom it is given. And God also begins again, showering love upon the child of an illicit union, and working to shape a future more in consonance with divine purposes than is the present.

THE BOOKS OF KINGS

A Still, Small Voice? (1 Kings 19:1-18)

"The still, small voice" has long captured the imagination of biblical interpreters. An appealing contrast with the "wind, earthquake, and fire" of the preceding lines has been the occasion for numerous attempts to set gentleness and calm over against the spectacular and miraculous. But, is that being true to the text?

> • Once an interpretation of a biblical passage has made its way into the regularly used materials of the synagogue or church, it is very difficult to hear anything else. For the sake of study it is helpful deliberately to take an angle of vision that cuts across traditional understandings. Whether it leads to a different interpretation or not, it will enhance one's understanding of the text.

One of the key questions is whether this text represents a stage in the history of prophecy, indeed in the history of God's ways with the people, or whether it is, more modestly, only an important incident in Elijah's ministry. Scholars have commonly moved in the former direction; it is questionable, however, that the text will bear such an interpretation.

Literary Matters

One of the more striking literary elements in the story is the exact repetition of the interchange between God and Elijah in vv 9-10 and 13-14. Thus, scholars have commonly suggested that vv 11-14 are an intrusion into the text, since one can read directly from v 10 to v 15 without skipping a beat. One needs to be careful here, however. Repetition is an important element in the Elijah–Elisha stories (cf. e.g., vv 5-8; 2 Kgs 2:1-8, and the virtual repetition of some of the Elijah stories in the Elisha cycle). Moreover, in terms of content, parallels with accounts of Moses at Mt. Sinai continue unabated into vv 11ff. It is also to be noted that God's question and rebuke (vv 9, 13) are much milder without vv 11ff. We shall see that the repetition has a very important role to play in the proper understanding of the story.

• The possible function of repetition in a text needs to be carefully considered before one resorts to explaining it as the result of multiple sources. This is especially important when the repetition is couched in identical or nearly identical language, as here. The passage needs to be judged on its own merits: does the repeated material stand in essential continuity with the style and content of the larger context; is there any good reason for considering it to be an addition apart from the question of style? Note that if vv 11-14 are removed, then the point of the original text is almost 180 degrees removed from the point as it now stands. Without vv 11-14, Elijah, like Moses, goes back to Mt. Sinai and gets a word from God like Moses got. With these verses, the difference rather than the similarity with Moses is highlighted. It is possible, of course, that an editor has inserted vv 11-14 in order to make the same point we shall suggest that the original author was trying to make.

Another striking aspect of this story is the number of parallels with the story of Moses. The central parallel is the appearance of God on Mt. Horeb (Sinai), "The mount of God" (cf. Exod 3:1; 18:5; 24:13). Other parallels are: the journey through the wilderness, both before (v 4) and after (v 15); the use of the number "forty" (cf. Exod 34:28; Num 14:34; v 8); the miraculous provision of food by God (vv 6ff.); the accompanying angel (Exod 23:20; vv 5, 7); the complaining in the wilderness (vv 4, 10, 14); the use of a cave, standing upon the rock, the Lord "passing by," and covering the face (Exod 33:21-23; 34:5-6; 3:6; vv 9, 11, 13); and the "earthquake, wind, and fire" (cf. Exodus 19). To be attentive to these parallels is crucial for the proper understanding of this text.

There is also a key difference to be found in this comparison. In fact, the importance of all the parallels may be to see this difference. Whereas for Moses the Word was closely associated with the "passing by" of God (Exod 34:6), and with accompanying natural phenomena (Exodus 19), here no Word from God is perceived in connection with these things. The Word which now comes is the same word that came before the theophany: "What are you doing here, Elijah?" (Cf. v 9 with v 13.) There is no distinctive word associated with the theophany. The instructions (v 15 ff.) come after the repeated interchange (cf. above), thus indicating that the theophany was not necessary for the giving of this word, though it was made more forceful as a result. Hence, the appearance in vv 11-13 has some function other than to announce a word (cf. below). This assumes that the "still, small voice" is not a word spoken, but silence; to this we shall return.

A final literary observation concerns the connections of this text with what precedes and what follows. Elijah's twice-repeated response is found in briefer form in 18:22, spoken before the miraculous resolution of things on Mt. Carmel. There it is made clear that the phrase "I, even I only, am left" has reference to prophets and not to faithful Israelites; the contrast is made with 450 prophets of Baal. That serves to underline the importance of the promise concerning Elisha as the prophet's successor (v 16) and explains why the beginnings of its fulfillment are related in the verses immediately following (vv 19-21, to be concluded in 2 Kings 2).

It is striking to note that two of the commands of vv 15-16 are not actually fulfilled by Elijah, but by Elisha (cf. 2 Kgs 8:7-15; 9:1-13). That the command and its fulfillment are not exactly correlated with one another is a somewhat unusual phenomenon in the deuteronomic history. (There is no reason to suppose an account wherein Elijah fulfills them has been lost.) Thus, it is likely that this inharmonious element is a very ancient one, accurately transmitted by the prophets' disciples. The fact that the stories allow God's commands to be carried out in such a general fashion suggests that, for the writer, there is nothing particularly new or striking about them. That is to say, there is nothing to suggest that the assigned tasks constitute some sharp shift in the nature of prophecy, e.g., that from now on Elijah is to be especially active in the political arena. Prophets were so involved from earlier times (e.g., Samuel; Ahijah). We will need to find some other point of significance for the commands, since Elijah actually fulfills only one part of them.

Retelling the Story

What would you do if Jezebel were after you? What would you do if you felt that, in spite of all your herculean efforts, you were making no real headway against the forces of evil in your community? What if you got to the point of thinking you were the only true "man of God" left in town—Yahweh's Lone Ranger?

We are invited to think of Elijah in terms very much like these. We are left thinking after chap. 18 that Elijah has made some progress in the conflict with the anti-Yahweh forces in Israel. But, chap. 19 immediately disabuses us of such thoughts. In an interesting look at Ahab's relationship to Jezebel, we are informed that, once he has told her (perhaps with the best of motivations!) all that Elijah has done, it is Jezebel that is in control of all that follows. Elijah is immediately informed that, rather than reversing royal policy, Jezebel is determined to kill him as he had killed the prophets of Baal.

In response to such a word, Elijah flees for his life. He heads south and, after leaving his servant in Beersheba, goes alone into the wilderness in the direction of Mt. Sinai. As we have seen, we now find him reliving two segments of the life of Moses: the trek in the wilderness and the experience at the mountain.

The wilderness journey (vv 4-8). The two most prominent items in this section are parallels with the two most significant aspects of the wilderness wanderings: the murmurings of the people and the continued care of God in spite of such complaints. Elijah's murmuring goes beyond that of the people in the wilderness in his wish for death. Nevertheless, its roots are comparable: God does not seem to be active in his ministry. But, even more, Elijah perceives that he has had no more success than other prophets have had: "I am no better than my fathers." In the midst of his self-pity, Elijah calls on God to kill him (no suicide is contemplated); better God than Jezebel.

In this time of despondency and despair, however, God does not follow through on what Elijah asks. The deity continues to provide for life, even when the impulses for death seem most pervasive. The prophet is incredibly sustained by God in the midst of his flight into self-pity.

This care provided by God retains a fundamental mysterious element. No conversation takes place between Elijah and the messenger; it is not even acknowledged by him that the sustenance comes from God. The gift is not seen to be anything unusual by Elijah; the entire incident is handled in a quite matter-of-fact way. Yet, it seems to move Elijah past his murmurings so that he resumes his trip to Sinai.

- Inasmuch as the narrative does not make anything "miraculous" out of this incident, we should not lift up that element either. Yet, because all of God's gifts are finally due to an extraordinary graciousness, the text does become a witness to the incredible providence of God. To ask into what a moving picture camera might have picked up, had some ancient reporter been there, is beside the point. The author is not writing history, but is seeking to show that the God of the wilderness wanderings is at work in comparable ways on behalf of this contemporary Moses. Whatever the details may actually have been, that point is made very clear.

The experience at Mt. Sinai (vv 9-18). It is not made explicit why Elijah would have wanted to make this long journey. It is conceivable that this reflects an ancient worship practice wherein the community made occasional treks back to this place so constitutive of Israel's life, but another factor seems more probable. It would appear to be a personal retreat to the traditional site of divine revelation; an attempt to return to a place of certainty in order to receive from God a repetition of the old revelation, and thus set him on his way again. If he alone is left among the prophets, and his life is threatened, then it would seem as if there is a need to return to the place of beginnings. Perhaps, amid all the accoutrements of the original Sinai experience, God could start a new people with Elijah at their head just as Moses had once done.

Once he arrives at the mountain (to which the cave is an allusive reference), the word of the Lord comes to him with no fanfare whatsoever: "What are you doing here, Elijah?" It is important to note that the emphasis in the question is on place, "here." The question contains an implicit rebuke; what is Elijah doing back here at Mt. Sinai?

Elijah responds in an oblique fashion, not directly answering God's question. He recalls the fact that he has been "jealous" for Yahweh, that is, he has refused any syncretism by insisting on the worship of Yahweh alone (note that the "jealousy" of God refers to exclusive devotion in Exod 20:5). By contrast, there has been apostasy on a massive scale on the part of the people: they have forsaken God's covenant (i.e., have been disloyal in their relationship with God), have thrown down God's altars (both literally and metaphorically), and have killed the prophets (cf. 18:4, 13). Elijah is the only one left, and his life is threatened. To the extent that this is a response to God's question, it would seem to be an indication of the desperate straits in which the community finds itself, and of the need for God to act once more as was done at Sinai long ago.

God's response is also indirect. Elijah is to stand "on the mount before the Lord." The scene starts out as if Elijah is going to receive some special insight like that received by Moses (cf. esp. Exod 34:1-6, where theophany follows upon the apostasies of Exodus 32, another Mosaic parallel to the present text). "And

the Lord passed by." In view of Exod 34:6, the expectation
would be that, as with Moses, this would be accompanied by a
special revelation. But what happens?

God actually does pass by, and spectacular natural events
accompany the passing. Rocks are broken in pieces by a wind
that rends the mountains, and this is followed, in turn, by
earthquake and fire. In connection with the manifestation of
each phenomenon, it is stated, "and the Lord was not in
this. . . ." The expectation is that the Lord would actually be
manifest, but it does not happen. It is almost as if God sets up all
the props for a typical theophany, building up the expectations of
Elijah with spectacular natural pyrotechnics. But then what
happens?

First of all, a deafening silence. Scholars have long debated
what the phrase "still, small voice" means. It is most likely to be
interpreted in terms of the moment of silence prior to a
revelation (see Job 4:16, for a comparable context). There are
three Hebrew words involved: "sound" or "voice"; "stillness" or
"silence"; "thin," "fine," or "small." The adjective modifies
silence, and would thus seem to be used figuratively in the sense
of "utmost." The phrase, "sound of silence," would appear to be
an instance of oxymoron, a contradiction in terms (e.g., a cruel
kindness, a gentle roar, jumbo shrimp, or the song made popular
by Simon and Garfunkel, "Sounds of Silence"). Thus, we would
suggest the translation, "the sound of utmost silence."

It is important to note that it is neither said nor implied that
God *is* in this sound, as over against the prior phenomena. It is
the moment prior to an expected appearance (as in Job 4:16).
When Elijah heard this (and after all the incredible noise, such a
silence would indeed have been strikingly audible), he responded in a fashion that suggests he was expecting a special
appearance of God (cf. Exod 3:6b; 33:22): he hid his face. Thus,
Elijah comes out of the cave with the expectation that he will now
be confronted, like Moses, with a glimpse of God and a special
word for the occasion.

But, then, in a moment of supreme irony, God simply repeats
the question that was asked prior to all the spectacle: "What are

you doing here, Elijah?" No special appearance, or word for him; rather, back to normal, to the way things had been prior to what had been anticipated as a new revelation for the moment of crisis. (It might be noted that, if one insisted on a translation of "voice, sound" that implied that a *word* was heard, then the only articulate word that is heard is the same question as was asked before, so the ironic point still stands.) Because of Elijah's obliqueness in his earlier answer, the question is quite appropriate once more. But, the irony intensifies the question. After all, Elijah has just witnessed these major convulsions of the natural order—a great show; everything seems set up for a great new revelation, but the same, simple question still comes: "What are you doing here, Elijah?" Thus, all of this which he has just experienced is not directly relevant for his continuing prophetic ministry.

Elijah's response is identical to what he had given before. Whether he catches the irony or not, he apparently believes that his concerns have not been addressed. It is as if he said: "All right, you may not have a new word for the future, but I still have this problem. What's to be done about it?"

The divine response has two basic components: a threefold command (vv 15-16), and a threefold promise (vv 17-18), which in turn invite a response of obedience and trust from Elijah.

God follows up the question about place with a command about place. Elijah is not to stay "here" at the mountain, he is to return home and to do certain things. What he does relative to these commands will address the concerns which he has expressed. Obedience to the Word of God is the first step toward a solution.

Elijah is to go to Damascus and anoint Hazael to be king over Syria, Jehu to be king over Israel, and Elisha to be prophet in his place. (Inasmuch as none of these individuals is said to have been actually anointed by Elijah or Elisha, it is probable that the verb, "anoint," is used in its basic meaning, "set apart.") These commands serve to provide some assurance to Elijah in his particularly desperate straits, as well as to indicate to him that the prophetic task should go on as usual; no special new revelation is needed.

The full word of God comes with the addition of the promise in vv 17-18, which is a word of assurance. These promises are fulfilled later according to the deuteronomic historian (see 2 Kgs 10:10), especially when Jehu wipes out, not only the family and household of Ahab (10:11), but all the devotees of Baal (10:25-28; cf. actions of Hazael in 8:28; 10:32ff.). There is, however, no record of any slaughter perpetrated by Elisha, perhaps because Jehu had finished the task in such fashion that no further action was needed by Elisha: no one escaped! (Note the conditional character of v 17 in our text.)

The problem presented by Elijah is, thus, addressed, not in terms of some special Mosaic-like revelation, but in being told to continue what he has been called to do as a prophet. Beyond the call to obedience, however, God responds with a promise: the devotees of Baal shall be slain, and there will be some seven thousand persons left in Israel who will not have bowed to Baal, thus providing a small but significant core to a continuing community of faith (this is the earliest clear promise regarding the remnant theme). Moreover, the Word of God will continue to have its spokesperson in Israel.

We return to the basic question posed at the beginning: Does this text represent a stage, or shift in the history of prophecy, or is it but an important incident in the ministry of Elijah? Our exposition has moved more in the direction of the latter interpretation. Yet, certain implications can be drawn for prophecy, and indeed all Israel, on the basis of Elijah's experience. Thus, e.g., it is clear that there can be no expectation of a Sinai experience again; a special revelation of that sort is a once-and-for-all event, and is not repeatable. God is not beginning again with some new Moses. Prophets will continue to receive and communicate the Word of God as they have for generations. Thus, in the history of prophecy, this text serves to cut off any idea that God will now take some new ways with Israel, or return to an older way: though the circumstances may seem to call for some radical shift in God's ways with Israel, it is affirmed that a prophet like Elijah remains the vehicle for God's word to Israel. No matter how bad the present situation may seem, God will find ways of moving through the crisis that do not entail beginning all over again.

This text could easily be appropriated by the Judean exiles. Their situation was in some ways comparable to that of Elijah. They were surrounded by communities who worshiped gods other than Yahweh. In addition, no doubt many exiles had fallen prey to idolatry. Like Elijah, the faithful were no doubt tempted to despair regarding the future. It may have seemed that there were only a few isolated loyal Yahwists left. The temptation may well have been to hope for a miraculous new beginning, a return to the certainty of the age of Moses. But, the Word of God for them is that one cannot escape from the problems of the present by longing for the past; that God continues to work through present leadership to preserve a community of faith that is far greater than one might imagine. While there may be continuity in experience between the present age and the age of Israel wandering through the wilderness, the divine response to the crisis will be different. There will be no new Sinai event, no special revelation, but rather a God who continues to work through existing vehicles to communicate, to elicit obedience, and to promise the elimination of evil and the preservation of the faithful.

In contemporary use of this text, certain avenues of interpretation are less true to it than others. There is nothing here to suggest that God will now be revealed in new ways, or that old ways of revelation are going to be discontinued. Thus, e.g., there are no suggestions that the natural or the spectacular or the violent or the miraculous are now to be given up (all occur in the Elisha narratives), while henceforth there will be a new emphasis upon the Word or the historical or gentleness or less obtrusive forms of divine activity. The emphasis is more on a theme like "You can't go home again." It is not possible to re-live or re-experience an old moment of certainty, even a constitutive revelatory experience like Sinai. In whatever crisis the (prophetic) community may be enduring, the way into a difficult future is to be obedient to the Word of God and to trust in its promises. God will see to the future of the community of faith, and even more, will see to the gift of continuing prophetic leadership for that community.

From One Leper to Another (2 Kings 5:1-27)

It is common to consider this pericope about Naaman and Elisha a miracle story. This is fostered by the fact that the lectionary text ends with v 14, ". . . and his flesh was restored like the flesh of a little child, and he was clean." One is left with the idea that it is the healing of Naaman toward which all else is driving. Those familiar with the story only in this form may not realize that the story is only half over. It is very important for understanding this text that the materials following the healing be taken into full consideration.

> ● It is not uncommon for lectionary series to cut up texts in this way. Those responsible for the divisions worked with correlations with NT texts, and even constraints of time and space (it's too long; it won't fit easily onto a bulletin insert). Verses 15-19 should be added to the reading, at least, or read from the pulpit if one is preaching on this text.

Some Opening Questions

Once again, viewing this text from the perspective of Israel in exile (Israel in almost any age, for that matter), the matter of immediate interest would have been the fact that Naaman was not an Israelite. In fact, he was in many ways parallel to their own Babylonian conquerors, among whom they lived. As a foreign army commander, he would have been responsible for defeating Israel in battle and taking them as slaves (such as the little girl of v 2). Moreover, an announcement, strikingly parallel to prophetic understandings of the role of Babylon in 687 B.C., is given at the beginning of the story: "By him the Lord had given victory to Syria." While no motive for such divine action is given in this text, the exiles might have assumed that the motive was the same one which accounted for their own defeat at the hands of Babylonia: disloyalty to God (cf. Jeremiah 21).

As a result of this observation one might be temped to suggest that the primary question lifted up by this text is: What ought Israel's relationship be to the foreigner or outsider? (Hence the text would be especially suitable for the mission emphasis of the Epiphany season for which this text is appointed.) Looking at the entire story, however, suggests that another question may be at the center of things: How can the people of *Israel* experience the healing that Naaman experiences? A sharp contrast is set up between the foreigner Naaman and the Israelite Gehazi, with "the leprosy of Naaman" coming to rest on Gehazi at the end of the story (v 27); it would appear that Jesus' use of this text in Luke 4:27 pushes in this direction as well). Nevertheless, even if this is the central way of approaching the text, implicit in this approach is the response to God, which it is possible for a non-Israelite to make.

Another possible issue has to do with the nature of proper prophetic leadership. Or, to put it more precisely: What shape should the ministry of the Word of God take in Israel? A contrast is set up between Elisha and his servant, Gehazi, in the way in which they relate to Naaman, particularly with respect to the taking of gifts and all that this implies.

It is sometimes suggested that the fundamental purpose of this text, as well as others in the Elisha (and Elijah) cycle, is to glorify the prophet. Yet, as we shall see, the prophet remains well in the background, so that such veneration seems a far-fetched approach, indeed. Such a direction would also serve to lift up the miracle for special attention, and that does not seem to be the case here. The contrast between Elisha and Gehazi would seem to stress the *way in which* the prophet does his work, rather than the spectacular nature of the result. Given the conflict among prophets in the late pre-exilic and exilic era of Israel's life (cf. Jeremiah 23; 28–29; Ezekiel 12–13), this text may well have been used to help sort out the issue of true and false prophecy. Such a consideration, moreover, does not have only sociological significance; it has implications for issues of leadership and the ministry of the Word of God.

Given these opening forays into initial questions the text raises, we need to take a closer look at some of the details of the text and see which direction they will push these more general focusing questions.

Literary Matters

First of all, some literary observations. The text begins and ends with a reference to leprosy (a literary technique called *inclusio*), with a foreigner having it to begin with and an Israelite at the end. This would seem to be an implicit criticism of the Israelite in the story; a judgment is passed on Gehazi (and his descendants!) because of a certain way of being a prophet. Yet, also implicit is that a Naaman-like experience would be possible for him, too.

It is striking to note who is named and not named in the story. Neither the king of Israel nor the king of Syria is mentioned (probably Jehoram and Ben-hadad). Only Elisha and Naaman are named in vv 1-19, while Gehazi is introduced in v 20. This serves to concentrate one's attention on the more important figures. Note also that Elisha is referred to as a prophet only in the first half of the story (vv 3, 8, 13), with "man of God" taking over at the point of the healing (vv 8, 14, 15, 20). This may serve to focus attention on the God who is ultimately responsible for what has occurred, rather than the person of the prophet.

Retarding elements serve to provide suspense as the story develops. This is seen particularly in the role given to the kings (vv 4-7; is this an implicit criticism of the monarchs, who often stand in the way of the work of the prophets?), and in the angry objection of Naaman (vv 11-13). The latter is a common feature in narratives where individuals are called to a God-given task (cf. Jer 1:4-9; Exodus 3–4; Judges 6).

The structure of the story reveals a very interesting progression. Verses 1-9 describe the movement of Naaman from Syria to Elisha's front door, the point where the central action of the story begins. Verses 19b-27 move away from the focal point of the story, but the focus is now on the activity of Gehazi, who moves from closeness to Elisha to a distance that approximates that of Naaman at the beginning of the story.

Verses 10-19a constitute the heart of the story, and an outline of this is especially pertinent.

v 10b—Command
v 10c—Promise
    vv 11-13—Objection of Naaman with its resolution
v 14a—Obedience to the Word of Command
v 14b—Fulfillment of the Word of Promise (healing)

v 15b—Confession of Faith
v 15c—Offering of gifts
    vv 16-17—Objection of Elisha with its resolution
v 18 —Request for pardon
v 19a—Blessing by Elisha

One is probably correct in seeing here the outline of a liturgy. It is tempting to suggest that it may represent a form of worship, which was used in healings (or a service of penitence? see Isa 1:16 and the metaphorical use of washing). Here, it would be applied to the peculiar circumstances of one individual.

- Those who are familiar with Christian liturgies might be tempted to suggest a similarity to the rites associated with the Sacrament of Baptism. One would want to be careful in any use of such parallels; it would not be appropriate to resort to language that suggests that this is some OT type of Baptism. Nonetheless, one may suggest that God's ways of working with people have common elements across the ages: the centrality of the Word of God (cf. v 14), the use of visible means, the importance of the (consequent!) confession of faith, and of the life to be lived.

It is not at all clear how this story is related to the larger cycle of Elisha stories. Naaman is never alluded to again, though the

Syrians are mentioned often. Gehazi reappears (cf. chap. 8), but with no apparent relationship to what happened to him in this chapter. Even the relationship of the Elisha stories to one another is difficult. There is no apparent chronological connection, and no coherent thematic structure that would appear to cut across the various stories and hold them together. One may yet be discovered, but at present it can only be stated that disciples of the prophet collected various stories, which had him and his activity as a focus. The purpose would seem not to have been that of lifting up Elisha as an especially venerable figure, but to show how important the prophets were in clarifying what Israel's history was about. With fully 40 percent of the book of 2 Kings devoted to the ministry of Elisha (even more than any king subsequent to Solomon), it was the apparent conviction of those who passed on the traditions that his activity had made a significant difference in Israel's history. They almost seem to be saying that without the prophets, Israel's history would not have been. It is also a way of saying that religious issues were the really important ones for Israel.

It is possible that there was once a source, independent of the present context, which could be called a "prophetic history," and that it contained these stories of Elijah, Elisha, and others. Yet, it seems more likely that the putting together of the various blocks of tradition was rather more gradual and haphazard, with a coherent history of Israel in something approximating the present form of Kings, emerging only very late in the redactional process. As has been suggested, while there may have been a significant point of redaction during the time of Josiah, it seems more likely that there was some working with the materials during that era (which left its impact here and there), but that the coherence that we presently see emerged only during the Exile from the hand of the deuteronomic historian.

Questions of historicity become especially prominent in the Elisha narratives, given the concentration of miracles that are performed. In fact, there is a greater concentration of such accounts in these narratives than in any other period of Israel's history, including the Exodus. How is one to understand this?

The chapter on historiography (above) needs to be appealed to here, as one attempts to sort out the various factors that need to be considered.

Retelling the Story

As a next step we need to work our way through the story pointing out a variety of features that enable us to get inside its central concerns.

> ● One very helpful way of preaching on materials of this kind is to interweave one's retelling of the biblical story with comments designed to point out how contemporary people of God can find themselves mirrored in the story. By contrast, to begin by talking about the story in a more objective way and then move to some application of the story, is to make the story into an object to be used rather than something with which one can identify as one's own story.

We are introduced to Naaman in v 1 in very striking fashion: "By him the Lord had given victory to Syria." This is astounding for a number of reasons. First of all, the victory was over Israel (cf. v 2), and thus the deliverance (lit., "salvation") is at the expense of the chosen people. What kind of sense does that make? There is a deep irony at work here. We are not told why God gave victory to Syria; there is no indication, in contrast to the later prophets, that Israel had sinned and hence the foreign nations were being used for purposes of divine judgment. But, it is precisely this God-given victory that enables the story to happen. Without an Israelite *defeat* at the hands of Naaman, he would never have heard about the prophet from his captured Israelite slave-girl, and there would have been no such story to tell, and the God of Israel would not have been acknowledged by this pagan foreigner.

Thus, the complexity of determining the nature of divine involvement in the life of the world is lifted up for our attention. Yahweh, the God of Israel, is at work in hidden ways, even in foreign and "pagan" places, and people like Naaman become involved in the activity without realizing it. Like Cyrus later, they may even become servants of the purposes of God without knowing that they are. Another ironic point is made. Naaman is successful in battle at the expense of Israel, only to find that it is at the hands of the defeated that healing will come to him as an individual (one might also note that it comes here not to the poor and weak, but to the strong). Thus, Naaman as hero, enemy, and foreigner all come into play and set key directions for the story.

Within v 1, further ironies are set in motion. For all of his power and status and heroism (note the emphasis on these things), Naaman is a "leper"; he cannot heal himself, and there is no known cure. The irony continues with the introduction in v 2 of the Israelite slave-girl (read a "little child" so that the parallel with v 14 can be caught). The future of this powerful man becomes dependent upon utter weakness. Even those who are slaves, without power in the common sense of that term, the seemingly little people, have an impact far beyond their status in life when they point to the word of God (here embodied in the prophet). G. von Rad points us in the right direction when he speaks of the hiddenness of God's ways and the plainness of his means.

A further irony is developed as the story continues with the introduction of the kings of Syria and Israel. Compared to the slave-girl, the kings are impotent. Perhaps, not being given names is intended to universalize the point. The little girl has the right word: You must go to the prophet! The king of Syria, however, though knowing exactly what the little girl said (v 4), misdirects the message to the king of Israel, thinking that the king has the power to cure the leprosy (v 6). The king of Israel compounds the impotence. While he knows he does not have the wherewithall to cure Naaman (unlike some kings, he at least does not admit to divine kingship), he interprets the entire matter in political terms ("He must be picking a fight"). Though he should have known where to direct Naaman, namely, to the prophet, he brings progress toward healing to a standstill. The narrator has, in the process, made a point: the prophet is a mediator of the word of God in the way that kings are not, and has power which kings do not.

The story is able to continue only because the prophet hears about the situation (v 8). Apparently, he is close enough to the court that he is privy to events of this kind. In any case, he indicates that the king ought not get desperate, for there is a solution to the problem. He asks that Naaman be sent to him "that he may know that there is a prophet in Israel." While this indicates that there is some concern in the story to lift up Elisha, it soon becomes clear that it is not the individual that is given focus, but the prophet as the bearer of the Word of God.

Naaman arrives at Elisha's front door "with his horses and chariots" and with some eighty thousand dollars in gifts in tow (cf. v 5b). The scene now sketched is also filled with irony. You have to imagine something like General MacArthur, in the aftermath of World War II, showing up in his limousine at the door of a Japanese household. Elisha sends his servant out to meet Naaman with a message; he does not even bother to show his face. In fact, Elisha does not put in an appearance until after the healing is complete. Thus, the prophet stays in the background, with the result that it is the word, rather than the person of the prophet, that is lifted up for special attention. This makes it clear that the story is not told to glorify Elisha; it is the word of God which emerges front and center. The prophet is not denigrated, however, for he is a crucial means through whom God works.

The message of the servant of Elisha consists of two parts: command and promise (see outline above). Bathing was commonly associated with attempts to ameliorate the effects of leprosy (see Lev 14:1-9); the *sevenfold* application of water (or ointment or other substance) was in line with medicinal practice in that part of the world at that time. It is interesting to note that the only element of the command to which Naaman objects is the need to wash in the Jordan river. There was nothing special about that water, particularly when compared to the beautiful and abundant waters of his own home country (a sharp contrast to the Jordan in both respects!). The heart of the objection of Naaman, however, relates to the fact that Elisha did not show up in person, engage in some hocus-pocus, and cure him on the spot!

This makes it clear that obedience is seen to be an essential element in the cure, as vv 13-14 also are at pains to point out. It is not the water, in itself, that is perceived to be the clue to the healing, as if the Jordan had some magical properties. It is the obedient response to "the word of the man of God" (v 14) when combined with the application of the watery means.

There is, however, one more important ingredient here beyond the command, the water, and obedience. It is the word of promise: "Your flesh shall be restored and you shall be clean." While obedience is not to be discounted, it is finally the word of promise which proves to be the efficacious element. It is a promise whose fulfillment is announced in v 14, "his flesh was restored . . . and he was clean" (this theme is prominent throughout the deuteronomic history, as we have seen).

● Such healing procedures are bothersome to many modern persons. It may bring to mind radio/TV evangelists who would charm diseases out of people in most unusual ways. As we have noted, however, Elisha keeps himself in the background in a way that these modern "healers" do not. Moreover, Elisha does not resort to unusual means. He makes use of knowledge of the healing arts that is available to him in his context (see above), and combines it with God's word of command and promise.

Part of our problem today is that we understand healing only in the context of human knowledge and therapy. If we allow for God's involvement at all, it tends to be in addition to or apart from the effectiveness of modern medical practice ("The doctors had done all they could . . . and then we began to pray"). We need to recall the ancient context, and the healings that took place through strange and "miraculous" techniques. Thereby, we might see that God makes use of the means available in every context, working through the medical knowledge of every age, in order to achieve good purposes for the people.

Keeping in mind the guidelines regarding historicity outlined in chap. 1 above, it would appear that no modern judgment can be made as to whether the miracle actually occurred.

It is to be noted that "little people" once again play an essential role in the episode. Given Naaman's rage at the way in which he was treated by Elisha, the story could have ended then and there. But, his own servants, pagans every one, persuade him to trust the word of the prophet and obey his command. And their only argument betrays intimate knowledge of their master. If Elisha had asked him to perform some heroic feat, somehow commensurate with his status in life ("a great man"—v 1), he would have had no difficulty. They perceive that it is the ease with which the command could be obeyed that is bothersome to him. In the end they appeal to his common sense and win their argument. And Naaman was restored, with the flesh of a "little child." One cannot help but refer back to the "little child" whose word started him on the way to this end. He has now become as she, one who trusts in the word of the prophet.

The healing is not the end of the story, as we have seen; it is probably not even to be seen as the climax. The latter may well come in v 15 with Naaman's confession. That the narrator recognizes its important place in the story is seen by the fact that Elisha now appears to Naaman for the first time.

What is the nature of the confession? The subsequent verses make the import of the confession more clear. In v 17, Naaman promises that he will not offer sacrifices to "other gods except Yahweh." The phrase "other gods" appears in the first commandment and frequently in Deuteronomy and in key passages in the deuteronomic history (e.g., Joshua 23–24; Judges 2; 2 Kings 17). One fundamental issue for the last of these sources was that Israel ought not (but often did) serve "other gods," and that the fall of the kingdoms had occurred because of such idolatry. The fact, then, that Naaman, a non-Israelite, promises not to worship other gods, presents a striking contrast to Israel. His confession that "there is no God in all the earth but in Israel" is similar to confessions found in other passages in the history (2 Sam 7:22; 1 Kgs 8:23; cf. 2 Kgs 1:3 ff.). It is striking that a comparable confession is found on the lips of both David and Solomon (and not found on the lips of Ahaziah, king of Israel, a contemporary of Naaman).

It would appear, then, that Naaman here enters into a faithful confessional tradition that goes back to David and Solomon, and stands in sharp contrast to most of the Israelites of the Elisha–Elijah generation. It is difficult to escape the conclusion that Naaman was intended as a model for contemporary Israelites who heard the story. And, one cannot help wondering whether the story would not have had its most powerful impact on the exilic generation, a people living among foreigners like Naaman? In this connection, it is startling to note that the confession has many parallels in the prophet of the Exile, Deutero–Isaiah (cf. Isa 46:9; 43:10ff.).

Upon making his confession, Naaman offers his eighty-thousand-dollar package to Elisha (v 15b). The latter, however, refuses the gift in the strongest terms (note the "As the Lord lives" of v 16), even though Naaman urges it upon him. This refusal has a much more important role to play in the narrative than is commonly recognized by the commentators. This is evident not least in the fact that vv 20-27 revolve around a contrary action on the part of Gehazi, the servant of Elisha. Yet, it is not immediately apparent from those verses why the attitude of Elisha is so crucial. For this we need to note the relationship between vv 16 and 17-18. Verses 17ff. develop as they do because of Elisha's refusal. That is, Naaman requests the loads of Israelite earth only because Elisha has rejected his gift ("If not . . . ," cf. JB: "Since your answer is No"). That Elisha has refused suggests that no credit for this healing is to redound to him; rather, it is the graciousness of God that is to be lifted up for attention. With the focus shifted from any ability of the prophet to the grace of God, Naaman should be able to draw fundamental insights into the nature of Yahwistic faith which he now adopts.

● One might be tempted to draw contrasts between Elisha's action and that of modern "healers" who accept major gifts from those whom they may have helped. The text speaks to this practice, but only to a point. That is, it does not oppose salaries, or the acceptance of gifts per se. It is a matter of discernment in each such instance as to whether acceptance will in any way obscure the grace of God. Given the fact that Naaman began his journey with the expectation that he might be able to buy his healing (v 5b), it became especially important here to disabuse him of any notion that, in fact, his healing had been bought. If that had not been done, his understanding of grace might well have been significantly diminished.

What insights does Naaman draw from the response? Now that the prophet has refused to take anything of Naaman's, the latter asks for something of Elisha's, namely, some earth from his plot of ground (the tie seems to be with Elisha, and not with Israel in general). Occasionally, scholars have suggested that Naaman here lapses into superstition, i.e., that he believes that it is only on Israelite soil that Yahweh is believed to be present, and hence only on such soil that Israel's God can be worshiped. However, the confession of v 15 (with its more universal understanding of God), and the fact that he would not have asked for the soil if Elisha had not rejected his gifts, suggest that another interpretation is necessary. Naaman realizes that he is not to sacrifice to "other gods," but to Yahweh alone. He desires that such worship take place at an altar built on the soil that he takes back with him. A *material* tie is thus provided to the community of faith, which Elisha represents. A solely spiritual relationship across the miles with this community is seen to be insufficient; there is need for those ties which are tangible, for the life of faith is not lived out in spiritual terms alone.

This understanding would seem to be reinforced by v 18, though it has a somewhat different focus. Naaman asks that Yahweh pardon him when he finds it necessary to accompany his master (the King of Syria) into the temple of Rimmon (a Syrian form of Baal) and participate with him in that worship. Again, some scholars have suggested that Naaman's faith already degenerates into syncretism. But, that would be to miss a very important insight. Here again is a recognition on Naaman's part that the life of faith is not an escape from the realities of life. The life of faith is always lived out in very ambiguous situations. There is no way that Naaman can remove himself from compromising situations, unless he escapes into an insulated community like the Rechabites (cf. Jeremiah 35). It is Naaman's insight into the nature of grace that enables him to recognize the freedom that the person of faith has in entering into life. This verse would be an excellent illustration of what Luther meant by "Sin boldly!" Again, the people of Israel in exile could see an especially pertinent word here.

Elisha's response, his second and last word to Naaman, is striking. He simply gives his blessing. It is interesting to note what Elisha does *not* say to him. He doesn't enter into legalisms, or even give ethical advice. He pronounces his benediction upon the life filled with ambiguities that Naaman sees before him. Moreover, he doesn't assure him of the pardon of Yahweh. This is simply assumed, given Naaman's perception. Even further, he doesn't suggest that Naaman now take up residence in Israel, so that he might not be confronted with such situations. He sends him back into his regular station in life, a life filled with ambiguities, but upon which the divine blessing has been pronounced.

● It is often very helpful, when interpreting stories such as this one, to observe as much what the narrator does *not* say as what he does say.

We come now to the final verses of the text. Gehazi does not agree with Elisha's decision to let Naaman get away without giving over some of the gifts which he brought; he has been "let off lightly" (JB). Thus, he pursues Naaman, and through a series of deceptions gets him to hand over a part of the treasure; Naaman responds gladly, and even has his servants help carry the gift back home for Gehazi. In v 25, Gehazi goes in and stands before Elisha just as Naaman had done earlier (v 15). This time, however, Elisha initiates conversation rather than his visitor; the time is not for confession of faith, but indictment and judgment. Elisha is aware of what Gehazi has done, in spite of the latter's attempt to hide it, and announces that the disease of Naaman will now rest on him for what he has done (this is not an example of clairvoyance, only a sensitivity with respect to a person whom Elisha obviously knew very well).

But what has he done to deserve such a judgment? One

possibility is that it is because of all the deceptions. Thus, he lies in saying to Naaman that Elisha had sent him, in giving him the song and dance about the two sons of the prophets, and in denying to Elisha that he had been with Naaman. Another possibility would be that Gehazi's problem is greed. This is the way that the Greek text understands v 26, followed by some modern translations such as JB. Thus, the difficult last half of v 26 is translated something like: "Now you have taken the money and garments and you can buy orchards, vineyards, etc." But, there is nothing in the text otherwise that would suggest this interpretation (or this translation); he even appears to bring the gifts back to Elisha's house (v 24 ff.), so that they were not for his own self-gratification.

The RSV appears to be correct in its emphasis upon the question of time. Elisha had not accepted the gifts because of how that might be interpreted by Naaman, that somehow his healing had been bought, and thus the grace of God might be diminished in his eyes. Thus, the indictment of Elisha zeroes in on just this point: "Was it a time to take. . . ." Gehazi had placed his own understanding of what a proper response ought to be above what God through the prophet had been about in the healing of Naaman. Elisha's comment about timing, then, would suggest: there may indeed be a time to talk about this kind of response, but not so with Naaman. The grace of God alone needs to fill Naaman's vision, and the freedom of the life of faith needs to be reinforced.

One might wonder about the harshness of the judgment given to Gehazi. Historically, it is difficult to determine just what may have happened. It is possible that Gehazi did contract leprosy, and that his previous behavior suggested an explanation for it. In any case it is used in the story to enforce a conviction: to obscure the grace of God is an especially reprehensible deed, since it contains the seeds of legalism and focuses on what people need to do, rather than on what God graciously has done. Whenever this happens, the faith is endangered. Thus, theological sins are seen as deserving harsh judgment just as is any other kind.

• One of the more important questions to ask when working with texts like this is: With whom in the text do I tend to identify? If one identifies with Elisha, then the force of the text will move one in the direction of mission to outsiders like Naaman. However, one will also be directed toward the importance of basing service on the grace of God. If one identifies with Naaman, then Naaman tends to become a type of what it means to be a person of faith, with movement from sickness, to repentance, to confession, and to the life of faith. But, even here the emphasis needs to be placed upon God's gracious act on behalf of Naaman, not on Naaman as an exemplar of faith, since he gets carried along that path at crucial points more often in spite of himself than because he has a sense of what ought to be. If one identifies with Gehazi, then the contrast with Elisha needs to be set up carefully, so that what finally emerges is not a word about deception or wealth, but about the importance of keeping the grace of God front and center in all one's relationships, particularly with those who may be new to the community of faith. Differences in type of leadership would also present themselves for consideration.

AIDS FOR THE INTERPRETER

General Works

While one authorized translation such as the Revised Standard Version may provide the basis for one's study, the use of two or three translations serves as an indispensable aid for interpretation. Annotated editions are the most helpful, and are available for the RSV (*The New Oxford Annotated Bible with the Apocrypha,* 1973), the NEB (*The New English Bible with the Apocrypha, Oxford Study Edition,* 1976), and JB (*The Jerusalem Bible,* 1966). Other helpful translations include NAB (*The New American Bible,* 1970) and the TEV (*Good News Bible, Today's English Version,* 1976).

The Interpreter's Dictionary of the Bible, 5 vols. (Nashville: Abingdon Press, 1962, 1976) is a very helpful reference work. See also, B. S. Childs, *An Introduction to the Old Testament as Scripture* (Philadelphia: Fortress Press, 1979).

Commentaries

Most of the commentaries on Joshua–Kings tend to be oriented to literary and historical problems, with few attempts made to grapple with theological issues. The Old Testament Library series (Philadelphia: The Westminster Press) is now complete: J. A. Soggin, *Joshua* (1972), *Judges* (1981); H. W. Hertzberg, *I and II Samuel* (1964); J. Gray, *I and II Kings,* rev. ed. (1970). The Cambridge Bible Commentary (Cambridge: Cambridge University Press) provides a brief, clear commentary: J. M. Miller and G. Tucker, *Joshua* (1974); J. Martin,

Judges (1975); P. Ackroyd, *I Samuel* (1971); *II Samuel* (1977); J. Robinson, *I Kings* (1972); *II Kings* (1976). Two volumes of The Anchor Bible (Garden City, N. Y.: Doubleday & Co., 1974) have appeared: R. Boling, *Judges* (1975); P. K. McCarter, Jr., *I Samuel* (1980). Compare also vols. 3 and 4 in *The Interpreter's Bible* (Nashville: Abingdon Press, 1956).

For a popular presentation of texts from 2 Kings, see J. Ellul, *The Politics of God and the Politics of Man* (Grand Rapids: Eerdmanns Publishing Co., 1972). Cf. also D. Gunn, *The Story of King David: Genre and Interpretation* (JSOT Supplement 6, 1978); *The Fate of King Saul: An Interpretation of a Biblical Story* (JSOT Supplement 14, 1980).

Special Studies

Special studies on the deuteronomic history abound, but the following may be cited as especially helpful. M. Noth, *The Deuteronomistic History* (JSOT Supplement 15, 1981); R. D. Nelson, *The Double Redaction of the Deuteronomistic History* (JSOT Supplement 18, 1981); R. Polzin, *Moses and the Deuteronomist: A Literary Study of the Deuteronomic History* (New York: Seabury Press, 1980); F. M. Cross, *Canaanite Myth and Hebrew Epic* (Cambridge: Harvard University Press, 1973); G. von Rad, *Old Testament Theology,* 2 vols. (New York: Harper & Row, 1962, 1965); W. Rast, *Joshua, Judges, Samuel, Kings* (Philadelphia: Fortress Press, 1978). M. Weinfeld, *Deuteronomy and the Deuteronomic School* (Oxford: Clarendon Press, 1972).

W. Brueggemann, "The Kerygma of the Deuternomistic Historian," *Interpretation* 22 (1968): 387-402; D. J. McCarthy, "II Samuel 7 and the Structure of the Deuteronomistic History," (JBL 84, 1965), 131-38; "The Wrath of Yahweh and the Structural Unity of the Deuteronomistic History," *Essays in Old Testament Ethics,* ed. by J. Crenshaw and J. Willis (New York: KTAV, 1974), pp. 97-110; H. W. Wolff, "The Kerygma of the Deuteronomic Historian," *The Vitality of Old Testament Traditions,* ed. by W. Brueggemann and H. W. Wolff (Atlanta: John Knox Press, 1975), pp. 83-100.